Responsibility without power?

Local education authorities and child protection

by Mary Baginsky

NSPCC

Cruelty to children must stop. **FULL STOP.**

About the author

Mary Baginsky is a Senior Research Officer in NSPCC's Research Group. After a brief teaching career she has conducted a variety of research and evaluation projects, mainly within an educational context but also those with a legal, criminological and social welfare focus. Amongst her current research interests are the role of the school in a multi-agency approach to child protection and counselling and support for children and young people.

Acknowledgements

Many people have contributed to this report. Darren Robinson, Georgina Ellis and Lucy Hadfield provided much needed administrative assistance in the early stages of the project. Sarah Webb, until recently Programme Development Manager at NSPCC, not only supported this project but gave me a great deal of support and encouragement with the range of work I am undertaking. Other colleagues within NSPCC – particularly David Coulter, Christopher Cloke, Julie Miles and Brendan Murphy – gave support and advice as the project progressed and the Head of Research at NSPCC, Pat Cawson, made valuable comments on an earlier draft.

I am also extremely grateful to Mary Palazzo (Cambridgeshire LEA), Carol Taylor (Hertfordshire Children, Schools and Families), Paul Saunders (Derbyshire LEA) and Ben Whitney (Staffordshire LEA), not only for the encouragement they gave but also for their useful and insightful observations on the questionnaire and the earlier draft.

However, the report was possible only because so many people in LEAs responded to yet another request to complete a questionnaire, which I think can be taken to reflect the importance they attach to the subject. I hope I have reflected their views accurately and fairly.

Foreword

Protecting young children is one of the most important duties that adults have to each succeeding generation. This valuable report fills out some of the answers to key questions because it is based on systematic enquiry.

Finding out what already happens is an essential precursor to improving practice. Disseminating such discoveries as widely as possible allows those charged with responsibility to examine what is being done locally and compare it with practice elsewhere.

Who takes responsibility for making sure schools are in a position to protect children and for monitoring and taking steps to improve the relationships between Social Services and teachers? These are just some of the questions asked and answered.

I hope very much that the findings of this enquiry will be distributed as widely as possible, so that the very best provision is available to the next generation, especially to those who are most vulnerable.

Professor E C Wragg, Exeter University

Contents

Executive summary

Background

Local education authorities (LEAs) are key partners in any attempt to protect children. The *Children Act* (1989) places a duty on the local education authority to assist Social Services departments acting on behalf of children *in need* or enquiring into allegations of child abuse. These duties are reflected in the guidance for educational services set out in Department for Education and Employment circular 10/95, *Protecting Children from Abuse: The Role of the Education Service*. Every LEA should also nominate a senior person within the LEA as lead officer with responsibility for co-ordinating policy and action on child protection for the schools it maintains. This designated officer should represent education services on the Area Child Protection Committee (ACPC), be involved in establishing local procedures (including arrangements for designated teachers) and be the LEA point of contact with Police, Social Services and other agencies. Circular 10/95 also recommends that all schools and colleges should have a designated member of staff responsible for co-ordinating action within the institution/service and liaising with other agencies, including the ACPC. Given the statutory and strategic role of LEAs in relation to the protection of children it is logical that schools and their LEAs should work together closely.

These responsibilities were placed on LEAs at a time when their role was being transformed and even their future status brought into question. As schools were given more autonomy their ties with LEAs were weakened. Although LEAs were clearly charged with the responsibility to support maintained schools in relation to child protection, it was an uncharted area for each to negotiate. An earlier survey had examined how LEAs were responding. It was evident that while there was a considerable level of activity in this area there were major obstacles to overcome. In view of the demise of grant maintained schools, the appearance of unitary authorities, the publication of two key documents,[1] and the continuing debate around the autonomy of schools and the responsibilities of LEAs, it seemed an opportune time to revisit the subject. It also seemed appropriate to look at how LEAs were being judged to fulfil their responsibilities in relation to child protection by examining the relevant sections of Ofsted reports on LEAs.

The questionnaire had already been distributed when the *Education Act* (2002) received Royal Assent. Section 175 requires LEAs to make arrangements for ensuring that the functions conferred on them are exercised with a view to safeguarding and promoting the welfare of children. It also places a responsibility on the governing bodies of maintained schools to make arrangements for ensuring that their schools operate in such a way as to safeguard and promote the welfare of their pupils. A proportion of respondents were followed up to collect their views on the section and on steps which would be necessary to support its introduction.

---

[1] *Working Together to Safeguard Children* (Department of Health et al., 1999) and *Framework for the Assessment of Children in Need and their Families* (Department of Health et al., 2000).

Survey

Questionnaires were sent to all designated officers with responsibility for child protection in the 150 LEAs in England, as well as to the relevant officers in the Welsh authorities and the Education and Library Boards in Northern Ireland. The results from Wales and Northern Ireland are reported in appendices in order to make the data available to those who will find the national data useful. Many of the key messages from the English authorities also apply to the other two countries.

One hundred and fourteen of the 150 LEAs in England responded to the questionnaire, which represents a response rate of 76 per cent.

- All but three of the 114 LEAs provided written guidance for schools on child protection issues, although only a small number made this available through a website.

- It was usually the named officer in the LEA with responsibility for child protection who represented the LEA on the Area Child Protection Committee (ACPC). In only 10 per cent of authorities was there more than one representative on the ACPC, somewhat lower than the 25 per cent where this was the case in 1997.

- There were some calls for a new senior post to be created, dedicated to ensuring that an LEA fulfilled its statutory responsibility in relation to child protection.

- In 72 per cent of responding LEAs schools were directly represented on the ACPC, and in a further eight per cent they were represented on sub-groups alone.

- *Working Together to Safeguard Children* (Department of Health et al., 1999) makes it clear that Social Services departments and ACPCs should offer the same level of support and advice to independent schools in matters of child protection as they do to maintained schools. So although LEAs do not have specific statutory responsibility for child protection in relation to independent schools it was relevant to ask if they considered that they had any responsibility. The majority thought they did, and the level of involvement with independent schools was higher than that reported in 1997:

    - Seventy-six per cent of respondents considered they had some responsibility and/or were involved with all or some independent schools in their areas (52 per cent in 1997).
    - Sixty-three per cent of these LEAs sent independent schools copies of all child protection mailings distributed to schools in the maintained sector (47 per cent in 1997).
    - Fifty-four per cent of them had provided some training for independent schools in their areas (14 per cent in 1997).
    - Forty-six per cent would be prepared to support independent schools in making a child protection referral to Social Services (24 per cent in 1997).
    - Thirty per cent of respondents referred to the advice provided by LEA officers to independent schools about child protection matters (27 per cent in 1997).

- The respondents were asked to say if their LEAs took responsibility for checking that LEA schools and independent schools had the following:

    - **Written policies on child protection**
      Eighty-five per cent checked maintained schools while 20 per cent checked independent schools.

- **Procedures in relation to child protection**
  Ninety-three per cent checked maintained schools and 26 per cent checked independent schools.
- **Designated teachers with responsibility for child protection**
  Ninety-eight per cent checked that maintained schools had such teachers in place and 23 per cent checked independent schools.
- **Measures to communicate the policy and procedures to staff**
  Eight-six per cent checked the maintained sector and 25 per cent the independent sector.
- **A nominated governor with responsibility for child protection**
  Sixty-six per cent checked this in maintained schools while only eight per cent of authorities did so in relation to independent schools.

- Ninety-two per cent of responding LEAs said that they provided a consultation service for their own schools in relation to child protection issues.

- Those responding on behalf of their LEAs were asked to say if they issued guidance, policies or procedures in relation to child protection in settings outside school used by pupils or students:

  - Thirty-eight per cent of LEAs did so in relation to work experience.
  - Thirty-four per cent did so in relation to other settings such as foreign exchanges, school trips and summer schemes.

- Ninety-two per cent included child protection training in their training programme for schools and 98 per cent of LEAs offered some training to the designated teachers in their schools, either directly or through the ACPC programme.

- The major difficulties identified in relation to the provision of child protection training for teachers were high staff turnover, the ability of schools to release staff, a shortage of supply teachers to provide cover, and funding.

- Most LEAs (85 per cent) provided some training either for all their teaching staff or for all those working in schools, although in most cases it was in response to a request from schools.

- There was some concern expressed about the difficulties involved in providing training for the large numbers of classroom assistants and learning mentors now working in schools.

- A higher proportion of LEAs (91 per cent) offered training to governors than they did to teachers who did not have the designated role. However, there were comments about difficulties in recruiting enough governors to attend training to make specific courses viable.

- The majority of LEAs maintained a database of the training designated teachers had received on child protection; and two thirds recorded the general level of training schools had received, where this had been provided by or through the LEA.

- *Working Together to Safeguard Children* (Department of Health et al., 1999) was prepared and issued jointly by the Department of Health, the Home Office and the Department for Education. It sets out how all agencies and professionals should work together to promote children's welfare and protect them from abuse and neglect, so it is important that everyone involved in safeguarding children is aware of the implications. Although 78 per cent of LEAs had at least taken account of this document in the child protection training they offered, only a minority of authorities had targeted all designated teachers for specific training.

- *The Framework for the Assessment of Children in Need and their Families* (Department of Health et al., 2000) provides a systematic way of analysing, understanding and recording what is happening to children and young people both within their families and the wider context of the community in which they live. There is an inbuilt assumption that the assessments will adopt a multi-agency approach. Although 73 per cent of LEAs had provided some relevant training, in most cases it was *ad hoc*, even more so than training provided in relation to *Working Together to Safeguard Children*. In many cases it amounted to little more than briefing sessions at meetings for head teachers and/or designated teachers. Just over 20 per cent of LEAs referred to multi-agency training on the *Assessment Framework*, usually conducted by Social Services (sometimes with Health and more rarely with Education). A small number of respondents referred to schools being well represented, but the majority stated specifically, or implied, that this had not been the case.

- Seventy-two per cent of respondents indicated that they issued specific guidance on informing parents when the school makes a child protection referral. Some of the documentation sent by LEAs gave schools very clear guidance about the procedures under *Working Together to Safeguard Children* and the *Framework for Assessment* in relation to circumstances where parental consent to a referral should be gained. Other documents were less than clear and some seemed confused. There was not always consistency in the advice given across LEAs or ACPCs.

- Just under half (48 per cent) of these LEAs were involved in other multi-agency training.

- Thirty-seven per cent of responding LEAs kept a record of the number of child protection referrals made by schools over the course of a year, although a few respondents made the point that the details of these may be recorded elsewhere, by the ACPC or Social Services. Twenty-eight per cent kept a record of outcomes.

- A third of LEAs recorded the number of child protection conferences at which schools were represented each year, and a quarter recorded the number of schools presenting written reports to conferences.

- Thirteen per cent of the LEAs provided funding to meet the cost of supply teachers to enable staff to attend conferences, although there were references from others to how this would be provided in the budgets devolved to schools.

- Sixty-two per cent of the LEAs issued schools with guidance in relation to children and young people displaying inappropriate sexual behaviours.

- Just over half (54 per cent) of the responding LEAs provided schools with specific guidance in relation to peer abuse, and nearly all those who did not thought it was a necessary step to take.

- Ninety-four per cent of responding authorities had recommended a procedure to schools for dealing with allegations of abuse against classroom teachers and head teachers.

- Fifty-two per cent thought there had been a need for the newly created regional posts of Investigation and Referral Support Co-ordinators, 32 per cent disagreed and 15 per cent were uncertain. Nearly every respondent was positive about having another officer with a child protection brief, but there was uncertainty about the nature of the role.

- Sixty-nine per cent had worked with unions and professional associations in the development of child protection policies and procedures, leaving a considerable number who had not.

- Respondents were asked if, in their opinion, the system for involving key agencies was working. Just over 75 per cent thought it was. The rest were divided equally between those who thought it partly worked, those who were not sure and those who believed it was not working. But even those who approved of the system thought its effective operation was challenged by a number of factors: limited resources; the threshold at which Social Services intervenes in relation to cases under Section 47 of the *Children Act*; Social Services' apparently limited response to Section 17 (children *in need* referrals); and general communication issues. The conclusion has to be that the majority believed either that a system is in place which is not working as intended or that a protective system for all children does not exist.

- There was concern about the availability of services for all children, both those *at risk* and those *in need* and about the ability of the current system to protect specific groups. Seventy-seven per cent of respondents thought that primary school children *at risk* would be protected, but only sixty-eight per cent thought this would be the case for secondary school children. In relation to children and young people *in need* only 47 per cent of respondents thought the system protected primary school children and the figure fell to 42 per cent for secondary children.

- Fifty-seven respondents were emailed to obtain their reaction to Section 175 of the *Education Act* (2002), which requires LEAs to make arrangements for ensuring that the functions conferred on them are exercised with a view to safeguarding and promoting the welfare of children. The idea of making LEAs and schools statutorily responsible for safeguarding and promoting the welfare of children was generally welcomed by just over half the 42 LEAs who responded to this request, although many of them were reluctant to be too positive without further details. The majority of respondents believed most schools did not need compulsion and that there were factors that stopped them from attending training and child protection conferences, such as difficulties making cover arrangements and a shortage of permanent and supply staff. These would have to be ameliorated before any significant change was possible.

- Respondents were asked to suggest what they thought LEAs would need to do to support the introduction of this legislation:
  - Review staffing and other resources devoted to child protection in order to make an appropriate allocation to meet the standard of practice required.
  - Create a LEA child protection post where one does not exist.
  - Promote a closer relationship between LEAs and ACPCs, possibly facilitated by the post holder suggested above.
  - Establish the means to respond to the expected demand from schools for support.
  - Provide an appropriate range of training to meet the needs of all teachers and others working in schools.
  - Review regularly the training received by designated teachers specifically and schools in general, especially as the data in relation to training of designated teachers, and support for newly qualified staff may be inspected.

- Respondents were asked to suggest what they thought schools would need to do to support the introduction of this legislation:
  - Recognise that all schools have a key responsibility in the area of child protection.
  - Plan structured training for all staff in relation to child protection.
  - Access the training and support offered by the LEA.

- Appoint a nominated governor for child protection who has received appropriate training.
- Report to governors annually on the management of child protection in the school.
- Identify a member of the school's senior leadership team to be the designated teacher with responsibility for child protection, even if a second designated teacher is appointed who does not hold such seniority, to allow that person the opportunity to effect change and influence attitudes.
- Allow the designated teacher sufficient time away from school to attend training, child protection conferences and other meetings.

- Respondents also had clear ideas about what they wanted to see in place as the legislation came into effect:

- Clear guidance from the DfES, written in consultation with experienced LEA and school personnel.
- A code of practice or a set of minimum standards to underpin the amendment.
- Earmarked funding, to support training and supply costs.

Ofsted reports on local education authorities

- Of the 133 Ofsted reports on LEAs which were examined 79 per cent (105) commented on the procedures the LEA had established in relation to child protection. Over the years the proportion of reports not referring to procedures has declined. So while a third of the 1999 reports failed to address LEA procedures, this fell to just over a quarter of the 2000 reports, and one tenth of those written in 2001. All of the 2002 reports examined covered the procedures in place.

- Only 41 per cent of the inspection reports referred to whether the LEA was meeting its statutory responsibilities. The proportion containing such a reference increased over the years until 2002, although not as significantly as in relation to procedures.

- The Ofsted reports contained numerous examples of single issues taken as indicators of success or failure in specific LEAs which did not appear in other reports. However, with the new *Framework* for these inspections there may be greater consistency and a sharper focus.

- In just over half (53 per cent) of the reports examined reference was made to the relationship between the LEA and Social Services at a strategic level and/or as part of a multi-agency approach to child protection. Only a minority of reports produced in 1999 and 2000 contained such a reference while the majority of the 2001 and 2002 reports did.

- Seventy-one per cent of the reports examined contained a reference to the training provided by LEAs for teachers. The number of reports containing such a reference showed a marked increase between 1999 and 2000, but over a quarter of the reports produced in 2001 still made no mention of training. However, the quality of the information recorded about training showed an overall improvement, although there was little consistency and the improvement was not universal.

Challenges

- There are challenges facing LEAs in meeting their responsibilities in this area which include:

- High staff turnover and limited resources in many Social Services departments that have resulted in higher thresholds for responses to schools' concerns.
- The establishment of a shared understanding of the roles of the respective agencies involved.
- The non-statutory nature of ACPCs and the variations in how they operate.
- Ambiguities surrounding the relationship between LEAs and schools.

The report concludes with a series of recommendations for both central and local government.

Section 1: Setting the scene

Local education authorities (LEAs) are key partners in any attempt to protect children. The *Children Act* (1989) places a duty on the local education authority to assist Social Services departments acting on behalf of children *in need* or enquiring into allegations of child abuse. Section 27 provides that any local authority may ask the LEA to help it fulfil its duty to provide support and services to children *in need*. Section 47 places a duty on any local education authority to help a local authority with its enquiries in cases where there is reasonable cause to suspect that a child is suffering, or is likely to suffer, from *significant harm*. These duties are reflected in the guidance for educational services set out in Department for Education and Employment circular 10/95, *Protecting Children from Abuse: The Role of the Education Service*. Like its predecessor (Department for Education and Science Circular 4/88) it recommends what should be in place to ensure each LEA, and each school, is in a position to meet its responsibilities.

In order to comply with the guidance contained within Circular 10/95 all schools and colleges and services should have a designated member of staff responsible for co-ordinating action within the institution/service and liaising with other agencies, including the Area Child Protection Committee (ACPC). As well as the statutory duties and guidance, schools have a pastoral responsibility towards their pupils and should recognise that pupils have a fundamental right to be protected from harm. However, those involved in schools in child protection work need to have knowledge and skills to enable them to fulfil their responsibilities. They need to be able to collaborate with other agencies and disciplines in order to safeguard the welfare of children and this requires them to have a sound understanding of the legislative framework and the wider policy context in which they work, as well as of local policy and procedures. Given the statutory and strategic role of LEAs in relation to the protection of children it is logical that schools and their LEAs should work together closely.

Every LEA should also nominate a senior person within the LEA as lead officer with responsibility for co-ordinating policy and action on child protection for the schools it maintains. This designated officer should represent education services on the ACPC, be involved in establishing local procedures (including arrangements for designated teachers) and be the LEA point of contact with Police, Social Services and other agencies.

As has been pointed out elsewhere (see Baginsky, 2000) these responsibilities were being placed on LEAs at a time when their role was being transformed and even their future status brought into question. As schools were given more autonomy their ties with LEAs were weakened and, although they were clearly charged with the responsibility of supporting maintained schools in relation to child protection, this was an uncharted area for each to negotiate. An earlier survey by the author was the first attempt to determine how LEAs were responding. It was evident that while there was a considerable level of activity in this area there were major obstacles to overcome. At a general level LEAs commented on the extent to which their powers to monitor and influence had been limited with the introduction of delegated budgets. More specifically they were concerned about how they would be able to sustain their child protection training programmes for education staff. In the years 1995–1996 and 1997–1998 LEAs in England had been able to apply for grants to support their work on child protection under Grants for Education Support and Training (GEST) funding. In both years this enabled senior teachers with designated responsibility for child protection to receive appropriate in-service training. Over 90 per cent of LEAs had made at least one bid for funding to support child protection training and most had been successful. Some authorities commented on how this had been used to pump-prime training, which they hoped would become an established part of their training programmes; others were concerned that they would not be able to sustain anything like the same level of training when the funding disappeared.

Since that survey was conducted in late 1997 grant maintained status has disappeared and LEAs have resumed responsibility for those schools, at least in certain respects. The number of unitary authorities has increased and the relationship with the originating authorities and their ACPCs has continued to evolve. In addition, two key documents have appeared. *Working Together to Safeguard Children* (Department of Health et al., 1999) emphasises the responsibilities of professionals towards children who are *at risk of harm* and clearly specifies the role of the LEA in promoting the welfare and protection of children. The stated intention of *Working Together to Safeguard Children* is to provide a 'national framework within which agencies and professionals at local level – individually and jointly – draw up and agree upon their own more detailed ways of working together'. The document was issued jointly by the Department of Health, the Home Office and the Department for Education and Employment[2] and replaced the previous version of *Working Together Under the Children Act* (1989), which was published in 1991. The other document was the *Framework for the Assessment of Children in Need and their Families* (Department of Health et al., 2000) which was jointly published by the Department of Health, Home Office and Department for Education and Employment. Since its implementation in April 2001 all referrals to Social Services are governed by the Assessment Framework. While Social Services have lead responsibility for assessments the underlying principle is that children's needs and their families' circumstances will require inter-agency collaboration to ensure full understanding of what is happening and to ensure an effective service response. The intention is to base this response on a thorough assessment and analysis of available information from all relevant agencies about a child and their family.

In the summer of 2002 the *Education Act* (2002) received Royal Assent. Section 175 requires LEAs to make arrangements for ensuring that the functions conferred on them in their capacity as local education authorities are exercised with a view to safeguarding and promoting the welfare of children. It also places a responsibility on the governing bodies of maintained schools to make arrangements for ensuring that their schools operate in such a way as to safeguard and promote the welfare of their pupils.

2002 therefore seemed an appropriate time to revisit the work of LEAs in relation to child protection. The survey[3] reported here returned to the issues examined in the earlier work and allowed an exploration of the effects of the changing relationship between LEAs and schools and the impact of practice developments such as the *Framework for Assessment*. It provided an opportunity to collect initial reactions to the statutory responsibilities placed on them by the *Education Act* (2002). It also seemed appropriate to look at another factor that has had an impact

---

[2]Subsequently, the Department for Education and Skills became a separate Government department in 2001.

[3]The questionnaires used in the survey are available from the author, email mbaginsky@nspcc.org.uk

on LEAs. Since 1998 LEA inspections have been conducted by Her Majesty's Inspectors (HMI) from Ofsted. As part of this review all these reports were examined to see what account the inspectors took of child protection.

Although the examination of the work of LEAs in this area was originally intended to update the previous work it has taken on additional significance in the light of national developments. The debate on the future shape of child protection is continuing following the Victoria Climbié inquiry and the submissions made to the Lord Laming's Inquiry. In the autumn of 2002 the Government announced that new bodies called Children's Trusts will be set up to oversee child care. Whatever decision is taken on the future of these services inter-professional work will lie at their core. At the present time LEAs are the key educational strategic partners. The success of future initiatives will depend in part on their ability to fulfil their responsibilities. Similarly, the extent to which schools are able to meet their existing responsibilities, as well as those imposed by recent legislation, reflects to a large degree the support they receive from LEAs.

Section 2: The survey

Process

An earlier survey conducted by the author in the late 1990s had provided the first set of data on the ways in which LEAs were responding to their responsibilities towards schools in relation to child protection (Baginsky, 2000). In the meantime several initiatives have impacted on both LEAs and child protection, some of which have been outlined in Section 1. It now seemed an appropriate time to return to LEAs to see what, if anything, had changed. Authorities in Wales and Education and Library Boards in Northern Ireland were included in the survey. Although most of the questions were the same there was some variation to reflect the differences that do exist between the three countries.[4] The responses from Northern Ireland and Wales are reported separately in Appendix 1 (Welsh findings) and Appendix 2 (Northern Ireland's findings). It would have been inappropriate to have merged the three data sets and repetitious to report them separately. Many of the messages that emerged from the responses of the English LEAs are reflected in the other two countries' responses. It should also be more useful to people working in those countries to have the data separated in this way.

All authorities were contacted to determine the name of the person with responsibility for child protection. In 38 per cent of authorities this was said to be a Deputy Director or Assistant Director of Education and in 37 per cent of authorities it was the Head of the Education Welfare or Social Work Service. In the remaining authorities it was most likely to be a Senior Education Officer from the section dealing with social inclusion or pupil services. However, not all the questionnaires were completed by these individuals. Where the responsible person was a Principal Education Welfare Officer or Social Worker or a Senior Education Officer they usually responded on behalf of the LEA. However, where that post was held by an Assistant or Deputy Director the questionnaire had usually been passed to a member of staff with more day-to-day contact with the issues it covered.

Respondents

One hundred and fourteen of the 150 LEAs in England responded to the questionnaire, which represents a response rate of 76 per cent. The questionnaires were completed by individuals holding a range of different posts including 41 Chief EWOs or equivalent, 19 Education Officers with specific responsibility for child protection, 13 Education Officers within social inclusion units and nine Deputy or Assistant Directors of Education. Other respondents included staff from pupil and schools services, special educational needs services and other sections within LEAs.

---

[4] NSPCC does not operate in Scotland but it would be interesting to replicate the study in that country. The questionnaires used to survey the Welsh authorities, produced in Welsh and English language versions, and the Boards in Northern Ireland are available from the author, email mbaginsky@nspcc.org.uk

Results

Written guidance

All but three of the 114 LEAs provided written guidance for schools on child protection issues. Only 20 respondents provided examples of the guidance they issued.[5] Fifteen of the responding authorities posted this guidance on their website, and eleven others were intending to do so within periods of six to 12 months.

Representation on Area Child Protection Committees

For the most part it was the named officer in the LEA with responsibility for child protection who represented the LEA on the Area Child Protection Committee (ACPC).[6] In only ten per cent of authorities was there more than one representative on the ACPC, which is considerably lower than the 25 per cent where this was the case in 1997 (Baginsky, 2000). This may reflect additional pressures on senior staff or the effects of re-organisations in many authorities resulting in fewer senior officers available to attend meetings. There were a few respondents who wanted to see someone with child protection experience, rather than senior status alone, appointed to represent their LEAs on ACPCs. Ideally they wanted to see a new senior post created dedicated to ensuring that an LEA fulfilled its statutory responsibility because the tasks were seen to be too important to be added on to an existing Principal Officer's duties. However, even in LEAs where there was a specific post that person did not necessarily represent the authority on the ACPC.

In 72 per cent of responding LEAs schools were directly represented on the ACPC and in a further eight per cent they were represented on sub-groups alone. There were comments about the difficulties involved in achieving this, or even attempting it, in a large authority. Various routes were used to obtain this representation. In some cases the LEA representative approached head teachers or other senior teachers they thought could make an effective contribution because of their particular interest or expertise in child protection. In other areas they were selected by their peers, or came through nominations from professional associations or they nominated themselves. There were LEAs where cluster groups of head teachers or designated teachers met and, in such cases, it was likely that this is where nominations would originate and how feedback would be facilitated. In areas where the heads or teachers had been self-nominated or had been approached, there were comments about how they did not have a constituency. Nor did they have a readily available audience for feedback. Some LEAs seem to have a more directive role in relation to child protection and schools, with more structured approaches to the representation of schools on ACPCs. Others are conscious that in most areas their links with schools have been weakened and do not see facilitating representation as appropriate.

---

[5] A more detailed analysis of these documents will be undertaken, but it is clear from a cursory examination that there is considerable variation in the documentation sent out to schools. Most of the material received had been updated in recent years and took account of the revised *Working Together* document. Very few documents made any reference to the *Framework for the Assessment of Children and their Families*.

[6] Or ACPC equivalent.

Responsibility for independent schools

The LEAs were asked if they considered that they had *any* responsibility for child protection in relation to independent schools.[7] *Working Together* (Department of Health et al., 1999) makes it clear that in relation to child protection the role of independent schools is the same as every other school. It goes on to state:

> *It is particularly important that independent schools (including independent special schools) establish channels of communication with local Social Services departments and ACPCs building on existing links with the local education authority, so that children requiring support receive prompt attention and any allegations of abuse can be properly investigated…. Social Service departments and ACPCs offer the same level of support and advice to independent schools in matters of child protection as they do to maintained schools.*[8]

Although LEAs do not have a specific statutory responsibility they are members of the ACPC and one of the more obvious sources of support and advice. Seventy-six per cent of respondents (n = 87) considered they had some responsibility and/or are involved with all or some independent schools in their areas. Many comments were similar to these:

> *Logically, no we don't have responsibility but we always copy independent schools into documentation and training opportunities.* (LEA Officer)

> *We send out copies of all documentation and guidelines to the independent schools in our area.* (Principal Education Welfare Officer)

Sixty-three per cent of these LEAs sent independent schools copies of all child protection mailings distributed to schools in the maintained sector, which is considerably higher than the percentage (47 per cent) doing this at the time of the first survey. Fifty-four per cent of them had provided some training for independent schools in their areas, although this was usually at a cost to the school involved; a further 16 per cent of LEAs were prepared to provide training. Again this was much higher than previously when only 14 per cent of LEAs had extended their training to non-maintained schools, although 44 per cent had been willing to do so. What these figures do not provide, however, is any information on the number of independent schools accessing this training. So more LEAs may be training staff from the independent schools but this could still be from a very small number of schools. However, one LEA was working with colleagues from Social Services on a training programme for independent schools.

Nearly twice as many LEAs (46 per cent) would be prepared to support independent schools in making a child protection referral to Social Services compared with the number prepared to do so in the last survey. Thirty per cent of respondents referred to the advice provided by LEA officers to independent schools about child protection matters, with a further 22 per cent mentioning their readiness to do so if a request were received. In the first survey the comparable figures had been 27 per cent and 36 per cent. Quite exceptionally one LEA expected all child protection issues arising in independent schools to be reported to it, and where an investigation was conducted they expected Social Services to report back to the LEA. Although no further

---

[7]One authority did not have any independent schools within its area.
[8]Paragraph 3.15.

details were provided it would seem likely that this was part of a planned, inclusive approach especially as designated members of staff for child protection in independent schools were invited to support group meetings, which some did attend. Not surprisingly those LEAs which considered they had some responsibility towards independent schools within their boundaries were significantly more likely to respond positively to those areas explored above. A small minority of the 26 LEAs that did not consider they had any responsibility towards independent schools did distribute relevant documentation (n = 4), offered training (n = 3), provided a referral route (n = 4) and professional advice (n = 8). The numbers more than doubled for those LEAs who would respond positively to a request for documentation, training or advice.

Only two respondents referred to independent-sector representation on the ACPC and another to a plan to secure this, but as they were not specifically asked for this information it may be more widespread. There were a few comments about the failure of independent schools to respond to the overtures made towards them, but overall it seemed as if most LEAs had made an effort to extend their services to the independent sector, some of which would be at a cost but not all.[9]

Monitoring policies and practice

The respondents were asked to say if their LEAs took responsibility for checking that LEA schools and independent schools had the following:

- **Written policies on child protection**

  Eighty-five per cent checked in relation to maintained schools while 20 per cent did so for independent schools.

- **Procedures in relation to child protection**

  Ninety-three per cent checked for maintained schools and 26 per cent for independent schools.

- **Designated teachers with responsibility for child protection**

  Ninety-eight per cent checked that maintained schools had such teachers in place and 23 per cent checked independent schools.

- **Measures to communicate the policy and procedures to staff**

  Eighty-six per cent checked in the maintained sector compared with 25 per cent in the independent sector.

- **A nominated governor with responsibility for child protection**

  Sixty-six per cent checked this in maintained schools while only eight per cent of authorities did so in relation to independent schools.

---

[9]Under section 157 of the *Education Act* (2002) the Secretary of State will prescribe standards that all independent schools will have to meet in a range of areas including the welfare, health and safety of pupils. DfES will consult on statutory regulations setting out the standards, and on the new inspection framework that will take account of them, early in 2003. The intention is that arrangements for child protection should be substantially the same in the independent and maintained sectors.

The proportion of LEAs engaged in each of these activities has increased since the last survey, but the increase has been most marked in relation to independent schools. Most LEAs do monitor the existence of policies, procedures and designated teachers in maintained schools, although there are authorities who fail to do so. In view of the new Ofsted framework it is unlikely that they will be allowed not to do so in the future (see Section 3). Just over two thirds of LEAs reported that they were checking that maintained schools had appointed a governor with responsibility for child protection, although a number of comments suggested some uncertainty about the requirement for such a person. An amendment to the *Education Act* (2002) specifically requires the governing body of a maintained school to make sure that the school safeguards and promotes the welfare of its pupils, which seems to indicate that such an appointment is presumed to be essential.

Although the level of involvement of LEAs with independent schools is reported to be much higher than it was a few years ago, it still leaves 16 per cent of LEAs who do not have any contact with independent schools in their areas. Even though the majority of LEAs have some contact with non-maintained schools, their comments reflected the fact that the contact is not systematic and is very dependent on the desire of senior staff in independent schools to engage with them on child protection matters. It is important that this is co-ordinated through the ACPC and that procedures are put in place to support independent schools in meeting their responsibilities to protect children.

Consultation service to maintained schools

Ninety-two per cent of responding LEAs said that they provided a consultation service for their own schools in relation to child protection issues. Nearly 50 per cent of respondents referred to the Education Welfare Service (EWS) playing a sole or major role in this. Traditionally the EWS has provided an important bridge between home and school, as well as maintaining close links with other agencies able to provide support. In view of the fact that in most authorities the major focus of the EWS is to secure high levels of school attendance, this work is in danger of being compromised. The history of the service means that some of the staff may well be qualified social workers, although with variable experience in relation to child protection. Many LEAs have Chief Education Welfare Officers (or equivalent) that are very experienced in this work, but this is not necessarily the case. Similarly there are LEAs that have specifically appointed some EWOs with a strong child protection background or have given interested individuals the opportunity to develop this expertise, but again there is considerable variation across authorities. The DfES guidelines, published on their website, make it clear that enforcing school attendance is the main responsibility of the EWS, but advising on child protection issues is listed as an important related duty which many LEAs clearly act on. But those appointed as EWOs are not usually required to hold a social-work qualification nor will they necessarily have appropriate expertise in child protection. The level of qualification, training and experience of their staff obviously impact on the ability of services to undertake core functions. However, as one senior officer pointed out, it is possible to address this with training in the same way as has been done for designated teachers, and many services do train their own staff on entry.

In just over half of the LEAs specifically mentioning the EWS there was also reference to another group or individual being available for advice. In most cases this was the lead officer for child protection. Where the Senior Education Welfare Officer did not hold this post, it was other LEA officers or trainers.

The feedback from experienced EWOs in contact with the researcher on different projects is that they now concentrate much more directly on attendance matters. They are no longer in a position to undertake social and welfare work that cannot be related to non-attendance and they are under too much pressure to provide families with services that should be provided by other agencies. However, much depends on the resources LEAs have put into child protection management and how the service is structured. In some areas designated teams of experienced officers concentrate almost exclusively on child protection work. In one authority the Ofsted inspection report on the LEA had criticised the failure of the EWS to target the high truancy level across the authority. The report on the re-inspection had commented favourably on how the EWS retains functions in respect of child protection and exclusions, but that the major focus was now on achieving a high level of attendance. In the meantime experienced officers, many with social-work qualifications, had left the LEA and those remaining were said to be unhappy with their posts after re-organisation.

It was not always clear from some responses how support was being accessed, and the impression was that the provision of support could be *ad hoc*, as reflected by the not untypical comments of these two respondents:

> *Schools know they can phone in here.* (LEA Officer)

> *Someone is always available to advise them.* (Education Social Worker)

However, whether it was the Chief Education Welfare Officer or another individual or group of individuals, the consensus from authorities that had dedicated posts was that they went a considerable way to providing a focus for child protection concerns and providing appropriate support.

There was a small number of LEAs that referred to other support structures or to related procedures that are worth noting. It may be that similar structures were in place elsewhere but the respondents failed to mention them. Only two replies specifically mentioned the logging of all child protection consultations. Two other authorities guaranteed a return call within one hour, while another did so within 24 hours. Only five respondents referred to making a mobile number available, although five LEAs referred to duty desks in the EWS that were open from 9 a.m. until 5 p.m. (in one case until 6.30 p.m.). Another authority provided the home number of the person offering support and this could be accessed at all times. In one area there was a hotline for schools straight to Social Services and, in a small number of instances, LEA staff said that schools were happy to ring Social Services' duty desk rather than come to them.

Ninety per cent of LEAs said that information about where to go for support and advice was included in the relevant documentation distributed to schools.

Policies and procedures relating to other settings

Those responding on behalf of their LEAs were asked to say if they issued guidance, policies or procedures in relation to child protection in settings outside school used by pupils or students. Only 38 per cent of LEAs did so in relation to work experience placements. It is perhaps surprising that there were no references to the DfES guidance *Work Experience: A guide for secondary schools* which covers child protection. Even fewer (34 per cent) produced any guidance in relation to other settings such as foreign exchanges, schools trips and summer schemes. It is possible that other parts of the authorities such as Youth and Community produce guidance for some settings but the *ad hoc* approach taken to this issue would benefit from more co-ordination.

Training

The majority of LEAs (92 per cent) include child protection training in their training programme for schools. Various patterns of provision emerged. In some cases all the training was part of the ACPC's rolling programme. In other cases the LEAs made no mention of the ACPC in this respect and referred only to their own training. Others described a mixture of training provided by the LEA in conjunction with other members of the ACPC.

One major change since the first survey was conducted is that there has been no specified funding for training in relation to child protection for some time. GEST (Grants for Education Support and Training) funding had specified child protection as an area that would attract a grant both in 1995–96 and in 1997–98. GEST funding was replaced by the Standards Fund, which is a collection of specific grants enabling schools and LEAs to achieve improvements in educational standards set out in agreed targets, particularly for literacy, numeracy, social inclusion and GCSE. It includes such programmes as the *National Literacy and Numeracy Strategies* and *Excellence in Cities*, and support for devolved capital spending by schools. The grants are paid to LEAs who are required to devolve most of the money to their schools. Almost all Standard Fund grants are allocated to LEAs on a formula basis and the Government expects LEAs to devolve grants to schools by a fair formula, in which case schools should not have to apply for grants. But the consequence is that because LEAs no longer hold on to the funds they are not able to plan courses in the sure knowledge that schools will send teachers.

Ninety-eight per cent of LEAs reported that they offered some training to the designated teachers in their schools, either directly or through the ACPC training programme. There was, however, considerable variation in what was provided. The most usual training involved a one-day course provided by the LEA alone or in conjunction with other agencies. There were authorities providing two-day courses with similar variations, and about one quarter referred to the three-day multi-agency training on offer to all designated teachers, either initially or as a follow-up to a foundation course. It was obvious that some authorities attempted to get as many designated teachers through a basic level of training as soon as possible, but with high staff turnover this could not always happen at the speed they would have wanted. Similarly, authorities that encouraged staff to attend two- and three-day courses were having some problems getting staff out of school for that period and some were experimenting with breaking courses into separate days or into two- and one-day blocks. One authority, however, had offered a one-day placement in a social work team and this had been taken up by 13 per cent of those designated teachers invited. They visited their local teams to observe duty social workers and followed through the decision-making process around the point of referral. The duty social worker was then invited back to shadow the teacher in school.

Only one authority referred to an annual conference for their designated teachers, but it could be that similar events were happening elsewhere and were not mentioned. The author has worked with schools in a number of LEAs and observed various daytime and after school meetings for designated teachers where both formal and informal training has occurred, but the respondents made no reference to these. They are often the venue for briefings on developments and new guidance, as well as offering peers an opportunity to exchange experiences and discuss practice.

Most LEAs (85 per cent) provide some training either for all their teaching staff or for all those working in schools, although in most cases it is in response to a request from schools and subject to other demands on those who would deliver it. A small proportion of LEAs attempted to run a rolling programme or had expectations that EWOs or others holding similar roles would work with schools in a defined area. Often LEAs expected designated teachers to train their colleagues and offer regular updates, on the basis of the input they had received. However, one respondent expressed his concerns about any expectation that designated teachers should automatically be expected to train colleagues:

> *Training in child protection should be sensitive, supportive and thorough. It is not like IT training and I don't think it should be attempted by anyone until they have thought through the issues.* (An Education Officer with Responsibility for Child Protection)

In that LEA a four-day training course was offered through the ACPC for prospective trainers.

There was some concern expressed about the difficulties involved in providing training for the large numbers of classroom assistants and learning mentors now working in schools. In some cases the expectation was that they would be included in other LEA or school-based training, but it is known that not all schools access or provide this as a matter of course. Although some LEAs and other agencies, such as Education Action Zones, have provided specific training for these groups there is a need for more training as they are people who may have more one-to-one contact with children in schools. Some comments reflected the concern that without appropriate training child protection procedures may not be followed and children could be placed at risk.

Three quarters of LEAs include peripatetic staff in their training but this is usually *ad hoc*, to a greater extent than training offered to all other school staff. Although there were a few references to specific courses offered by some LEAs and Social Services, in most cases it would require these teachers to access other appropriate training offered by schools, LEAs or others. But as these teachers usually work across a number of schools, and are not usually working on INSET days or at the end of the day when whole staff training often occurs, they may not be aware of the importance of accessing training unless they are specifically targeted. Some LEAs take very seriously their responsibility for preparing newly qualified teachers to meet these responsibilities. But too many do not have the resources to do so or choose not to. It also has to be recognised that LEAs are powerless to force schools to send their teachers on this training. In a survey of over 1100 newly qualified teachers only 17 per cent had been on a child protection course run by their LEAs (Baginsky, 2003). Schools are another source of training, but again only 20 per cent of these newly qualified teachers had received any child protection training in their schools.

A higher proportion of LEAs (91 per cent) offer training to governors than they do to those teachers who do not have the designated role. In some cases governors are invited to child protection awareness training offered to other groups; in others it is a component of the generic training offered to all governors, but most LEAs offer or have offered specific training. However, there were comments about the difficulties encountered in getting enough governors to attend to make specific courses viable. This response was just one of ten referring to cancelled child protection courses for governors in the past year:

> *Despite offering sessions the last two have been cancelled due to lack of support. We do (as a Unit) attend the Governors Training Days (generic training) which take place*

> *twice a year on a Saturday and we try to advertise our wares then.* (An Education
> Officer with responsibility for child protection)

In view of the *Education Act* (2002), which will make governing bodies of maintained schools responsible for ensuring that their functions relating to the conduct of the school are exercised with a view to safeguarding and promoting the welfare of children who are pupils at the school, the demand from governors for training is likely to increase significantly.

The majority of LEAs maintain a database of the training which designated teachers have received on child protection; and two thirds record the general level of training which schools have received, where this has been provided by or through the LEA. There was general agreement that it was not possible to be certain about any training provided to schools by their own designated teachers or where schools may have engaged other trainers, such as from a voluntary agency, to provide school-based training.

Most LEAs were fairly confident that schools recognised the importance of releasing designated teachers for training but, since the demise of the GEST funding, the take up of training by others, and by designated teachers for more advanced training, had declined.

There are variations in funding assessments across LEAs. There are those that ring-fence a proportion of Standard Fund money and offer training to schools in the expectation that they will attend, and there are those who hold no funding centrally and expect schools to pay for training. There are also LEAs and ACPCs providing training at no cost to the schools, but this does not necessarily extend to paying for cover to enable teachers to attend. In some areas this did not seem to affect attendance, while in others it was identified as a reason for poorer attendance. Some authorities are adapting their training plans accordingly and expect their own staff to deliver as much training as possible during INSET days and in twilight sessions at the end of the school day. Others are facing up to the reality of schools not being able to find or fund supply teachers or pay for training by trying to provide as many free courses as possible, in the hope of improving the general level of child protection competency. A typical response was:

> *I am the Child Protection Officer but I do not have a budget for training so I rely on*
> *schools attending my free courses or those offered by the ACPC.* (An Education
> Officer with responsibility for child protection)

DfEE circular 10/95 allows LEAs to decide if they will retain central LEA funding for supply cover for designated teachers on in-service training courses or attending child protection courses or delegate these funds to schools. One third of LEAs identified the failure to provide ring-fenced or specific funding as a reason for fewer teachers attending child protection training, but nearly as many identified the problem of staffing in schools alongside finding supply teachers to cover for those attending training. Sixteen per cent of LEAs said they would pay for the supply cover required. Where this was not the case it was most likely because the budget had been devolved to the schools already. When they did not it would obviously fall to the school to do so or arrange some other form of cover. But even when LEAs paid supply costs there were still difficulties because of the scarcity of supply teachers in many areas:

> *Our schools have more money than say five years ago and funding does not appear to*
> *be an issue. Finding supply teachers for cover is the problem. Paying them isn't.*
> (Assistant Education Officer)

The question of cover appeared to be a bigger problem for primary schools where there was less flexibility and small staff numbers; it is easier to arrange cover from other members of staff in a large secondary than in most primary schools. In many cases these problems meant training was occurring increasingly in twilight sessions and where other in-service time was available. However, some respondents said that it was much harder to get staff from secondary schools to attend training, possibly because they saw these schools as having to respond to a much wider agenda. In one authority the allocated budget was always under-spent, even though courses were well publicised. The respondent thought that this would change with the implementation of the requirements of the *Education Act* (2002) discussed later in this section:

> *I am sure that this will mean that this budget will now be grossly overspent. In fact it was the most powerful tool for me in persuading Heads that they should make a commitment to all this.* (Head of Child Protection)

There is also the question of the priority that schools give to child protection, and even if a course is free and accessible there has to be the will to attend. In some authorities no one from as many as 30 per cent of schools had attended child protection training in the past four to five years. The response to non-attendance in some areas is to approach the school and encourage attendance, but this also depends on the availability of staff to undertake the contact. In the long term respondents wanted child protection training to be given a higher profile by the Department for Education and Skills. They believed that one of the major barriers to training was the fact that there had never been a clear connection made between the imperative to raise attainment and the emotional and physical security of children:

> *An injection of social exclusion money would reflect the importance of child protection to schools. In the end schools have to make it a priority for themselves and funding through social exclusion which went beyond a year might help us arrive at a more mature position.* (Chief Education Welfare Officer)

The various patterns that emerged, both in relation to the provision of training and how it was supported, are inevitably tied to the way in which the LEA has chosen to meet its responsibility in relation to child protection. Where specific posts had been established or where the EWS had retained an expertise in child protection, even amongst only a proportion of the EWOs, they were likely to play a key role in delivering LEA training and identifying training needs. Sixty-four per cent of respondents also referred to their contribution to ACPC training budgets, which supported multi-agency and other training. However, small LEAs really were struggling to find the most appropriate response. Contributions to their ACPCs were a drain on funds for the relatively small number of education staff accessing their training, and even funding a full-time trainer was not a practical step. But even some larger authorities seemed to have few resources at their disposal. In one LEA there was one trainer delivering designated-teacher foundation training, as well as INSET training to 450 schools, which made it a very difficult task to manage.

Some ACPCs were also trying to offer training on shoestring budgets, usually by trying to do as much as possible in-house and using people involved in their sub-groups. However, in some areas where the contributing agencies were able to support more vibrant training programmes – sometimes with an inter-agency training co-ordinator – there were fewer comments about falling numbers of attendees and even reports of substantial waiting lists. Some authorities have also responded to the pressures on schools by increasing the amount of in-service training they will undertake, as well as introducing twilight and half-day courses. However, a very few respondents saw devolving the training budget to schools as advantageous in that it gave schools the chance to employ other trainers, rather than rely solely on the expertise available within the LEA or ACPC. This may have been because they could not meet the attendant demand. However, it is known that some authorities recommend that their schools use trainers who have links with, or are approved by, the LEA so that training is known to meet certain standards and reflects the authority's policy and procedures.

A laissez-faire approach – devolving training budgets to schools and relying on schools to pay for attendance at courses, make their own arrangements and pay for cover – generally resulted in fewer courses, more cancelled events and reduced numbers being trained. Where money was retained by LEAs, where ACPCs took an active role in training staff from the various agencies, and where there were specific staff within the LEAs who had a prominent and respected role in relation to child protection, few problems were reported. However, some difficulties remained: finding teachers to cover classes to release colleagues for training, encouraging teachers to be out of school for more than one day when they often have responsibility for large classes, an exam-oriented curriculum and other aspects of school life. There were also schools with low child protection awareness. In some cases this was said to be the result of a perception that they would not have children who were abused or who were *at risk*. In other instances there was some concern that certain schools were part of faith or similar communities which believed they were in a better position to deal with most problems and did not consider they required the assistance of outside agencies.

Despite the fact that Ofsted inspection reports on LEAs increasingly comment on the proportion of designated teachers who have attended training courses (see Section 3) it is not clear what action an LEA is able to take if schools fail to attend. Most LEAs continue to make a considerable effort to ensure all designated teachers have received appropriate training. A few respondents were concerned that a significant proportion of schools have not sent anyone on child protection training for too long, but the majority are managing to maintain this training with at least a reasonable level of success. However, the difficulties examined above mean that this is not always an easy task. There were real concerns expressed about the feasibility of extending training to all those working in schools, both teaching and non-teaching staff.

Working Together training

Working Together to Safeguard Children (Department of Health et al.,1999) was prepared and issued jointly by the Department of Health, the Home Office and the Department for Education and replaces the previous version of *Working Together Under the Children Act* (1989), published in 1991. It sets out how all agencies and professionals should work together to promote children's welfare and protect them from abuse and neglect, so it is important that everyone within these agencies is aware of the implications. Although 78 per cent of LEAs have at least taken account of this document in the child protection training they offer, it is unclear what proportion of their schools would have attended training since its introduction. Newly appointed designated teachers would obviously receive it, as would those attending refresher courses. But lack of recent training could leave a proportion of schools with a perspective out of step with other agencies. Given that there were LEAs who responded that there had been a marked fall in the representation of schools at multi-agency training, it is of some concern that it would be at such sessions that much of the more detailed *Working Together* training and briefing would take place. A minority of authorities have targeted all designated teachers for this training, often given by staff from Social Services, and in some cases the programme will continue into the next academic year. More positively, most LEAs referred to having updated their policies and procedures in the light of *Working Together* and other documents, so many schools will have received updated training materials and/or information packs even if teachers have not been trained. It is, however, of some concern that just over 20 per cent of LEAs responded that they had not provided any training to reflect the introduction of *Working Together*. This respondent was not alone in questioning why it had taken so long for the DfES to give appropriate guidance:

> *The fact that the DfES have now taken more than two and a half years to respond to the new Working Together guidance and update their own guidance - it took them six years to respond to the Children Act. They seem more concerned with keeping the Teacher and Head Teacher unions happy about allegations against staff.* (Chief Education Welfare officer)

Framework for the Assessment of Children in Need and their Families

The *Framework for the Assessment of Children in Need and their Families* (Department of Health et al., 2000) provides a systematic way of analysing, understanding and recording what is happening to children and young people within both their families and the wider context of the community in which they live. In this way an assessment can be made of whether the child is *in need*, is suffering or likely to suffer *significant harm*, and the actions that are required. The intention is to enable informed professional judgements to be made about which services would best meet the needs of this particular child and family. The *Framework* is built on the assumption that delivering services to children *in need* is a corporate responsibility that depends on all local authority departments, health authorities and community services. Local authority Social Services departments, working with other local authority departments and health authorities, have a duty to safeguard and promote the welfare of children in their area who are *in need* and to promote the upbringing of such children, wherever possible by their families, through providing an appropriate range of services. Its success depends on close collaboration between professionals and agencies working with children and families.

There is an inbuilt assumption that the assessments will adopt a multi-agency approach, but it is evident that more training has been given to Social Services than to other agencies. Detailed evidence from research in three local authorities (Baginsky, forthcoming), and from discussions with LEA personnel and teachers in many other areas, is that while Social Services departments will rightly remain the lead agency, other agencies have had little preparation to assume potentially more proactive roles. There have been difficulties in implementing the *Framework* in many areas, although not in all, but delays and uncertainties have probably had an impact on the training of other professionals. This was reflected in a number of comments similar to the one made by this respondent:

> *Very little has happened. Social services are still unclear about the expectations and there has been no clear commitment to any change in inter-agency procedures at senior level in other agencies.* (Education Officer)

The survey provided the opportunity to obtain a clearer picture of how LEAs were responding to the challenge, either on their own or as part of their ACPCs. Although 73 per cent said there had been some relevant training, and a further three per cent were planning to offer training, the accompanying comments gave the impression that in most cases it was *ad hoc* to an even greater extent than that provided in relation to *Working Together to Safeguard Children*. In many cases the *training* amounted to little more than briefing sessions at meetings for head teachers and/or designated teachers and in some cases it was restricted to EWOs and Educational Psychologists. Just over 20 per cent of LEAs referred to multi-agency training on the *Assessment Framework*, usually conducted by Social Services (sometimes with Health and more rarely with Education). A small number of respondents referred to schools being well represented, but the majority specifically stated, or implied, that this had not been the case. In a few instances, where training had not been offered, schools received a briefing paper about the changes which, given their complexity, may have been of limited use. It is possible that in those authorities where nothing has yet happened the LEAs are waiting for a clear steer from the ACPC or for Social Services to be more explicit about their expectations.

At a Department of Health conference in September 1996 to examine the response of local authorities to the refocusing initiative, Michael Little of the Dartington Social Research Unit commented that they 'were not all running at the same speed'. Moira Gibb, the then Director of Social Services in Kensington and Chelsea, replied that many departments had not yet 'got their running shoes on, still less made it to the starting blocks'. The same comments could equally well be applied to the introduction of the *Assessment Framework*.

In view of these responses in relation to training it is surprising that about half of the respondents (49 per cent) thought the introduction of the *Framework for Assessment* had had an effect on the LEA's involvement in child protection. Those that did were reasonably positive about what is beginning to be achieved. They focused on the intention to identify more clearly children's needs, to adopt more structured approaches to a real multi-agency perspective in assessment, to act within more stringent time constraints, and to arrive at a clearer understanding of thresholds adopted by Social Services and the boundaries within which schools must work when making referrals. However, even amongst those who thought there had been positive effects there was a repeated recognition of how much more could be achieved if the agencies had the time to understand each other's practice and if more training occurred:

> *The Framework was adopted in September 2001 when the new multi-agency handbook was published. Yes, it has had an impact at an operational level. There were plans for multi-agency training, but insufficient resources were available at the time, but this is about to be taken up again.* (A Chief Education Welfare Officer)

While some respondents welcomed what they viewed as a more stringent approach to the referral process – one that required schools to accept more responsibility for their actions – they were aware that this had caused some problems. There was an appreciation of how difficult it has been for some schools to engage parents in the assessment process, to approach them to discuss and gain their consent to the referral for assessment. Although respondents thought that this engagement with parents was welcome, at least in theory, there were many who appreciated the additional strains placed on schools as a result. The *Framework* is very new and the speed of its introduction has varied across the country. Not all social workers felt confident about its implementation and in some cases schools had been given confusing and conflicting advice. Many Social Services departments are under-staffed, which aggravates this and means they do not have the capacity to undertake proactive work with schools. These comments were typical of many observations made by respondents:

Schools feel unsupported in that the criteria for the threshold for child protection now seem too severe. They are left with vulnerable children in school with inadequate resources to address needs. (LEA Officer)

Individual social workers are sometimes confused by the dual procedures and have refused to accept some Section 47 issues without going through Section 17 procedures that may be inappropriate. (LEA Officer)

Seventy-two per cent of respondents indicated that they did issue specific guidance on when and how to inform parents when the school makes a child protection referral. In examining the material sent by LEAs it was apparent that some documents gave schools very clear guidance about the procedures under *Working Together to Safeguard Children* and the *Framework for Assessment* in relation to circumstances where parental consent to a referral should be gained. Others were less than clear and some were positively confusing. Neither was there always consistency in the advice given out by LEAs or ACPCs. This was more evident in the responses to the survey than in the documentation sent by LEAs. Some areas seemed to have made significant progress in the refocusing of services for families, with the emphasis on working with parents whenever possible. Others stressed the needs of the child over those of the family and took a more cautious approach to circumstances where parents should be consulted about a referral.

There is a need for clear guidelines to schools on when to approach parents for consent prior to making a referral to Social Services.[10] Although professionals should usually discuss any concerns with parents or carers, and where possible seek their agreement to make referrals to Social Services, this should be done only where such discussions would not place a child at increased risk of significant harm. This is in line with *Working Together to Safeguard Children.*[11] *Safeguarding Children: A Joint Chief Inspectors' Report on Arrangements to Safeguard Children* (Department of Health, 2002) recommended that the Lord Chancellor's Department, the Home Office and Department of Health should ensure that there is clear guidance provided to all agencies under their respective responsibilities on the implications of the *Data Protection Act* (1998) and the *Human Rights Act* (1998) and other relevant law, in respect of sharing information about children where there are welfare concerns.

Other multi-agency training

Just under half (48 per cent) of these LEAs are involved in other multi-agency training. Apart from basic child protection these courses cover domestic violence, safeguarding children in whom illness is fabricated or induced, drug and alcohol abuse, preventative models of care, looked after children and many related areas.

Child protection referrals and outcomes

Just over a third (37 per cent) of responding LEAs kept a record of the number of child protection referrals made by schools over the course of a year, although a few respondents made the point that the details of these may be recorded elsewhere, by the ACPC or Social Services. Even fewer (28 per cent) kept a record of outcomes.

---

[10]The Department of Health is currently carrying out work on this issue.
[11]Paragraph 5.6.

Child protection conferences

Child protection conferences are central to the effective inter-agency management of child protection. They are called for all children who have been the subject of a child protection investigation for whom there remain suspicions that they have suffered, or are at risk of suffering, significant harm and there are unresolved child protection issues.

There should be sufficient information and expertise available – through personal representation or reports. Briefing reports from social workers are expected, but reports from other agencies are also valuable (see 5.62 *Working Together to Safeguard Children*, Department of Health et al., 1999). The conference will use this information to make an informed decision about the action needed to safeguard the child and promote his/her welfare, and to make realistic proposals for taking that action forward.

Most LEAs do not send a representative to conferences unless there is an allegation against a member of staff, although there is a small number of LEAs always represented by their child protection staff. Not surprisingly, these tended to be authorities employing more staff with a specific child protection remit. Otherwise it is hard to see how it would be possible to be represented at more than a few conferences. In a few authorities the liaison officer may attend where it is a particularly complex case, where a conference is held during the school holidays, where a child has special educational needs or to support newly appointed designated teachers. However, schools are expected to attend and in many instances so are Education Welfare Officers and, where appropriate, Educational Psychologists. If schools find it impossible to attend they are expected to submit a written report. However, only a third of LEAs have the annual figures on the number of conferences where schools were represented, and even fewer (25 per cent) keep a record of the number of schools presenting a written report to conferences. Some authorities referred to the decline in the number of conferences where schools were represented, while others said attendance did not seem to be a problem, but without accurate figures it was very difficult for some respondents to be confident about the reality.

In other contexts schools have referred to the difficulty they face in attending conferences when they are given very short notice or when they occur in the school holidays, so they may not even be aware of them (see Baginsky, forthcoming). Once again a significant factor is providing cover for a member of staff in the course of a school day. Only 13 per cent of LEAs provide any funding to meet the cost of supply teachers, although there were references to how this would be provided in the devolved budgets. Nevertheless, there was a fairly widespread recognition that this would be one way of facilitating more schools to attend conferences.

Inappropriate sexual behaviour

LEAs were asked to state if they issued schools with guidance in relation to children and young people who display inappropriate sexual behaviours. Sixty-two per cent said that they did, but in a number of instances they were referring to ACPC guidance to all agencies or to advice that would be available to schools. Typical were these respondents who said that guidance was available to schools, but schools would not necessarily know about it:

> *ACPC joint protocol between agencies has been circulated recently. Schools will not be aware of it if asked.* (LEA Officer)

It is available via the (LEA's) Child Guidance Department. (LEA Officer)

It is referred to in the procedures as an incident. Schools are encouraged to telephone Social Services or the EWS to discuss concerns. (Senior Education Social Worker)

In a number of authorities the guidance is integrated into the child protection procedures issued to schools. Where this was the case and where the documentation had been provided most were very clear and accessible, while others were difficult to locate and less explicit. There may well be good guidance developed specifically for schools which was not submitted, but it is an issue which causes a great deal of apprehension in a school, particularly the first time an incident is identified. This makes it all the more important that schools are provided with clear advice. With few exceptions all authorities currently without this guidance responded that they thought it necessary. All respondents recognised the importance of supporting schools:

Schools are keen to keep young people but are let down by a lack of agreed assessment or service provision. (LEA Officer)

It is important that written guidance is part of this support strategy. A number of the authorities developing their guidance submitted reflective and interesting comments:

Guidelines will probably be helpful but it is something that could be based upon a national template with flexibility for local amendment. (LEA Officer)

Our guidelines only touch on this and it needs further development. We are awaiting a multi-agency approach. Whilst the LEA would always look to provide risk assessment/additional support/resources to protect both the child who is sexually inappropriate and protect other children we struggle to do this properly, given the absence of a multi-agency protocol. Sometimes we don't even get told when other agencies are working with children who have allegedly committed very serious offences such as multiple rape. (LEA Officer)

Peer abuse

Just over half (54 per cent) of the responding LEAs provide schools with specific guidance in relation to peer abuse, and nearly all those who did not currently do so thought it was a necessary step to take. However, without further details of what authorities were providing it is not possible to say how many were defining this as guidance on dealing with bullying. Indeed, some authorities who claimed to provide guidance referred to their documentation on bullying, while some of those who claimed not to provide it referred to their materials on dealing with bullying, but believed that something was needed beyond that. A number of authorities said they would welcome guidance on the areas that should be encompassed.

Curriculum materials

LEAs were asked if they had encouraged schools in any way to teach personal safety skills in response to the duty of schools set out in circular 10/95 and reinforced by the national framework for PSHE. Nearly a third of respondents (32 per cent) failed to make a response to this question or did not know if anything had happened, and 13 per cent said that they had not taken any steps to support schools in this way. In a small proportion of LEAs the respondents had worked with others to provide appropriate training. However, these figures may not, in fact, accurately reflect what is going on in their schools as it is possible they were not aware of curriculum developments. While the majority of respondents did say that the LEA supported this aspect of the curriculum, not surprisingly the support usually came from another section of the LEA such as the advisory service, principally the PSHE advisors and/or the Healthy Schools initiative. An exception was the LEA where the Education Child Protection Service had produced its own materials to link with the LEA framework for PSHE. It was introduced to PSHE co-ordinators with the support of the PSHE service. The two services worked closely together to ensure a joined-up approach, by co-operating over the development of materials and the identification of schools where it would be introduced. The materials were sold to schools at cost price, with the option of accessing accompanying training for which there was no charge.

Allegations against staff

Ninety-four per cent of responding authorities had recommended a procedure to schools for dealing with allegations of abuse against classroom teachers and head teachers. In most cases this amounted to circulating ACPC guidelines, sometimes with attachments specifically for schools, including charts of the relevant course of action, contact numbers and referral points.

Nearly three quarters of responding LEAs (74 per cent) said they had taken steps to reduce the risk of a member of school staff being involved in an allegation of abuse. In some cases this amounted to additional training, either by LEA staff or specialist consultants, but in other authorities various committees looked at the problem or co-operated with the newly appointed Investigation and Referral Support Co-ordinators (see below). Where the subject had been addressed in training this was sometimes in a child protection context. In other authorities it was covered only on training related to behaviour management and restraint of pupils.

Investigation and Referral Support Co-ordinators[12]

The posts of Investigation and Referral Support Co-ordinators were introduced in 2001. The then Secretary of State for Education announced that he wanted a network of Co-ordinators to give guidance on alleged incidents, in the wake of certain high profile cases. Twenty-six Co-ordinator posts were created. Funding was agreed up to the end of March 2004. The intention was to establish this network across England with each post holder being responsible for a group of LEAs and employed by a lead authority in each grouping. The Co-ordinators' first priority was to work with senior LEA officers who had responsibility for child protection and personnel issues and with ACPC partners to review existing procedures. Where appropriate, they were to put in place local arrangements aimed at reducing the time taken to deal with allegations of abuse made against teachers and other staff in schools. This was intended to help reduce the stress caused by allegations. The Department for Education and Employment wanted Co-ordinators to have strategic responsibility to improve consistency in the way these cases were dealt with and help LEAs provide appropriate support to teachers, schools and governors. The Department also wanted them to have strategic responsibility for supporting schools in identifying children *at risk* and encouraging consistency, and for disseminating good practice, in

---

[12]The official title of these post holders is Investigation and Referral Support Co-ordinators but they were also known as Regional Child Protection Co-ordinators, and it was this title that was used in the questionnaire.

relation to child protection arrangements in schools.

Most of these Co-ordinators have been appointed but at least one cluster of authorities has decided not to make an appointment and several others had failed to appoint by the summer of 2002. Only two respondents (one per cent) failed to answer this question, which means that a small number were answering without having any experience of working alongside a Co-ordinator.

Respondents were asked if they thought there had been a need for the introduction of these posts. Fifty-two per cent thought there had been, with 32 per cent taking an opposing view and 15 per cent being uncertain.[13] Nearly every respondent was positive about having another officer with a child protection brief, but there was uncertainty about the nature of the role.

A more complex spectrum of opinion emerged when the accompanying comments were analysed, a far higher proportion expressing a negative view of how the post was currently constructed. In the minority (n = 18) were those who commented that the work being undertaken by those in post was valuable in bringing clarification and consistency to the way in which allegations were dealt with:

> *I have been involved with the steering group and although at first I did not feel there was a need I now realise that every area deals with allegations in a different way and I feel it needs a national approach.* (Assistant Director of Education)

There were also a few who saw the Co-ordinator as potentially able to improve child protection practice in general because they would have oversight of authorities in one region and could facilitate discussion and change:

> *They will be able to encourage consistency of approach and share good practice between authorities and the work they are doing should enable a better response from governors regarding allegations against staff if the DfES provide clear guidance.* (Chief Education Welfare Officer)

> *Although our systems work reasonably well it is good to have someone in post with an overview of more than one authority.* (LEA Officer – Child Protection)

The hope was that they would facilitate the introduction of consistency across authority boundaries, led by national guidance on allegations from the DfES.

However, the largest group either thought that there was a purpose in these posts but did not think that the current emphasis on allegations was necessary or were uncertain because of the current priorities of their local Co-ordinator (n = 58). The Co-ordinators had spent a significant proportion of the time since appointment working on an audit of policies and procedures on, and incidence of, allegations. Although they had usually established good links with their authorities, where discussions had ranged widely across topics beyond allegations, there was still a feeling that they were answerable to a DfES agenda when there was a lot of local work in need of support. This group of respondents would prefer to see the role develop

---

[13]Two respondents failed to make any response to this question because they were unaware that anyone had been appointed, which accounts for the remaining one per cent.

into one which did identify and disseminate good practice across an area:

> *I have answered yes but only if the ultimate aim is to improve child protection practice*
> *in general, not if it is to reduce the time taken up when there is an allegation against*
> *a teacher.* (LEA Officer – Child Protection)

> *Yes but only if the remit is broadened.* (Chief Education Welfare officer)

There were repeated references to the importance of the work that LEAs already did in relation to child protection and for this to be more widely recognised and supported. They welcomed the Co-ordinators but only if they were able to contribute to a broader child protection agenda. At the present time there were very few references to this happening. Instead, many respondents would probably agree with this comment:

> *I thought the post would help me push forward with better audit and impact analysis*
> *of the service, but there seems little stomach for it and less interest from the DfES.*
> *Those who are less happy with the post seem able to ignore it for the most part.*
> (Assistant Director of Education)

The responses of those who did not think the posts were needed echoed much of what is set out above, but without anticipating that their introduction would have positive aspects. The introduction of Co-ordinators was seen as both a *knee jerk* reaction and as a sop to the trade unions, to demonstrate to them that action was being taken to counter the reported rise in the number of allegations against teaching staff. They were not the only respondents to say how seriously their authorities already took their responsibilities in relation to allegations. However, some admitted that in the past there had not always been a consistent response to allegations. Some referred to the expertise within authorities and were concerned that this could be under-valued. But respondents opposing the introduction of the posts would have preferred other avenues to be explored before the posts were announced without prior consultation. With the increased attention from ACPCs, a higher level of multi-agency co-ordination and a greater expertise developing within LEAs, support was sought in the form of additional resources directly for LEAs to be able to work with schools and raise their awareness of what constituted good practice, rather than through a post which covered up to ten authorities.

There were comments from both those who approved of the new post and those who disapproved about the high quality of many individual Co-ordinators. But there were additional comments about the appointment of some individuals who appeared to lack an understanding of the reality of school-based work. A number of respondents also referred to what they considered to be the inappropriately low level at which the job had been graded compared with the senior officers in authorities with whom they would be expected to work. In addition there were those who perceived the postholders' brief as having originated in the DfES rather than from within the authorities with whom they worked. However, this has to be balanced by the comments of respondents who felt that the Co-ordinator covering their authorities had made a significant attempt to understand local issues and respond appropriately.

It is, perhaps, not surprising that these posts should have elicited such a mixed response. The regional brief, combined with the perceived emphasis on allegations, means that by their very nature these posts would face challenges. While the majority of respondents viewed them positively, because of the pressures under which they operate, they would have welcomed a sharper focus on the child protection aspect of their brief. If this had been the case the negative reaction from the minority may have been tempered.[14]

Unions

A majority of LEAs (69 per cent) have worked with unions and professional associations in the development of child protection policies and procedures, although this still leaves a considerable number who have not. In those authorities where it happens consultation appears to be part of the normal procedures in relation to any initiative that may impact on schools. However, some respondents pointed to specific issues where there had been consultation such as in the development of policies on the restraint of pupils, and handling allegations against members of staff and subsequent investigations. A number specifically referred to revisions required as a result of the *Framework of Assessment*.

Effectiveness of the system to protect children

Those at risk of significant harm and those in need

Respondents were asked if, in their opinion, the present system for involving key agencies was working. Just over 75 per cent thought that it was, with the rest divided equally between those who thought it partly worked, those who were not sure and those who believed that it was not working. Those who responded positively believed that the system worked well when effective communication occurred and everyone followed the agreed ACPC procedures:

> *Of course we do not always agree or act appropriately but the system is effective if used properly.* (LEA Officer – Child Protection)

> *It works because we make it work. The designated officers in each agency meet regularly and monitor communication across the authority.* (Assistant Director of Education)

> *The inter-agency working arrangements have worked well to date. There is a range of multi-agency working groups and Education is very much a key player in the ACPC and on sub committees. Education and Social Services Children's Services have now joined together to form one department. The consequence is that the system should become even more effective.* (A Chief Education Welfare Officer)

In some cases it was said that the system worked well because the authority was small and this facilitated communication; in other cases the respondents said significant effort had been put into making it work. It would be interesting to have more details of how this was measured or audited.

A number of replies referred to having made a realistic response in view of the resources available:

> *In general it works well, but there is not room for complacency and any guidelines/procedures can be improved. Resources and problems of recruitment are factors which result in the system failing.* (LEA Officer)

---

[14]In the closing months of 2002 the Independent Schools' Council appointed Regional Representatives to liaise and work with the Investigation and Referral Support Co-ordinators.

About a third of those who were satisfied that the system was working still referred to the challenges posed by limited resources: issues around the threshold for Social Services to intervene in relation to cases under Section 47 of the *Children Act* and their perceived insufficient response to Section 17 (children *in need* referrals); and general communication issues:

> *I feel we all work together. There is always room for better communication but roles are more clearly understood now, which helps. The lack of social workers does not help.* (LEA Officer)

> *It works better once cases have met the child protection threshold and conferences happen. Staff appear to network well and work together in planning for the future.* (LEA Officer)

> *As ever the focus is on when it does not work. Yet every day I witness good inter-agency practice which doesn't make headlines. Shortage of staff, i.e. social workers at key points, means the system may not function. This does not mean the system is wrong.* (Education Social Worker)

While the majority of respondents were confident that the system in place worked, or could be made to work, they recognised the challenges and, in some cases, they suggested solutions. So, for example, there were repeated references to schools not always believing that they had received an appropriate response from social workers. Staffing problems in Social Services, different cultures in the two agencies and differing definitions of what constituted a child protection case were identified as problems. Regarding solutions, obviously more staff on the ground would be universally welcomed but sometimes the deployment of existing staff was reported to have produced improvements:

> *Schools want to know that their concerns are listened to. If they are making a referral they want to know what has happened to it. Social Services have guaranteed that they will get back to them within two hours to talk through the nature of that referral. A school will want to talk with someone if they are concerned or unsure. They also want to know what is happening subsequently. I believe practice has improved because of the greater interchange between individuals. It is not perfect but the two agencies understand what the expectations are and no one should be able to hide behind excuses.* (LEA Officer)

> *Social Services have now provided a service description for all schools with a named social worker as a contact. Schools have experienced difficulties with Social Services due to a 60 per cent increase in child protection referrals last year, particularly for those children in need but on the cusp of suffering significant harm. The LEA designated officer and Social Service's child protection officers attempt to improve understanding and resolve difficulties.* (LEA Officer)

There was the expectation that if the level of training could be sustained and extended so as to raise awareness of other agencies' responsibilities and limitations, and if *Working Together* and the *Assessment Framework* could be fully implemented, the system would work even more effectively.

Those who took the opposing view, or who were uncertain about whether the system was working, focused on the same issues. However, instead of seeing them as aspects requiring attention to make the system function more effectively, they viewed them as indications that the current system was not working:

> *The system relies on full staffing quotas and sufficient resourcing, neither of which is present in Social Services. School staff get very frustrated that their expectations, raised in training and in guidance, are treated as no further action by Social Services when they strongly believe them to be child protection cases (never mind in need). In this area Social Services staff are often inexperienced and have had little child protection training but are dealing with child protection referrals.* (A Chief Education Welfare Officer)

> *The system does not work because it relies on the foot soldiers. You can have excellent relationships and levels of co-operation between the senior officers of different agencies but they are not doing the day-to-day work. Teachers' main priority has to be the education of the children in their schools. This does not mean they do not take their responsibilities for the welfare of children seriously, but they are not the experts. They are told in training that they should be watchful for the indicators of abuse but when they have concerns they do not necessarily get a reaction from Social Services because a threshold has not been crossed. Thresholds are the natural response to the available resources and the judgement of individuals in duty teams. The complexity has increased now we have children in need assessments. The system may stand a chance of working if you had child protection experts in schools. Many designated teachers for child protection have developed an expertise but do not have the time; others still see their role as one of passing on referrals to someone else. No, it will not work based on the current set up.* (A Senior Education Social Worker)

These respondents frequently mentioned the child protection route as being the only way to secure services for children and young people, and that children *in need* either got short shrift or nothing at all. Their criticisms of the system usually rested on the way it was tied to the allocation of resources and gateways to services.

However, in both groups, there was some concern about the availability of services for all children, both those *at risk* and those *in need*. They referred to Government policy decisions to refocus services on the family and raise the thresholds triggering a child protection case. Some respondents feared that this had shifted the focus from the child to the family to the detriment of the child:

> *Everything is child focused but only if you can get past the parents. Children should have a right to an assessment if their circumstances deem it appropriate. Parental permission is tantamount to asking a burglar for permission to offer counselling support to his victim. Children in need are only in need if their parents agree.* (LEA Officer)

Even those who obviously welcomed this realignment emphasised the need to constantly monitor the system from a multi–agency perspective to make sure that children were protected and not put at greater risk by making it more difficult to enter the child protection system.

When respondents were asked to express their opinion on whether, as a society, there was a system for protecting specific groups their responses were more cautious. It was a deliberately provoking question to give respondents the opportunity to reflect further on their response to whether the system was working. While 77 per cent of respondents believed that the system in place protected primary age children *at risk of significant harm* and 69 per cent believed it did so for secondary age pupils at risk, the figures fell below 50 per cent in relation to children *in need* in both sectors. Before the implications for children *in need* are explored it is worth noting the further evidence of a widespread belief in the system: three-quarters of respondents believed there was at least an adequate system for protecting primary age children who were *at risk* and only a slightly lower proportion believed this was true for secondary age students. This is in line with research indicating that children are usually well protected when there are serious child-abuse concerns. However, it is still necessary to recognise that approximately one quarter of respondents did not share this belief completely or at all.

Table 1: Views on the system's ability to protect children – England

Group	Yes	No	Other*
Children of primary school age who are *at risk*	88	77%	10
of significant harm	*8%*	*16*	*15%*
Children of primary school age who are *in need*	54	47%	37
	32%	*23*	*21%*
Children of secondary school age who are *at risk*	78	68%	18
of significant harm	16%	18	16%
Children of secondary school age who are *in need*	48	42%	41
	36%	25	22%

★ Includes those who expressed uncertainty, referred to there being too much variation and those who failed to respond to this question (ten per cent of respondents).

Most of the additional comments reflected concerns about the effectiveness of the system, even from those who had responded that a system was in place to protect all groups. The conclusion has to be that the majority in fact believed that either a system is in place and not working as intended or that a protective system for all children does not exist. *Working Together* clearly sets out the procedures for multi-agency work, the *Assessment Framework* provides the practical tool for its implementation, and the refocusing initiative should mean that work is directed to support all children *in need*. But it seems there is still a long way to go before this can be achieved. The differences in response in relation to children and young people *at risk* and those *in need* were usually accounted for by recognising that resources were still targeted towards the more acute cases requiring protection. While it was recognised that services should have been refocused to give due regard to prevention, there were many respondents who questioned whether the objectives of the initiative could be achieved. Some of the challenges were the same as those identified in relation to the effectiveness of systems to keep children safe. The pressures on Social Services, because of shortfalls in staff and other resources, often meant that children *at risk of significant harm* would receive a response while that those *in need* may not, even if the policies, procedures and training had been put in place:

> *I believe we have the systems in place but because of the shortage of social workers*
> *some of the thresholds seem rather high before they trigger help for children who are*

neglected or otherwise in need. (LEA Officer)

We have the system in place backed up by local procedures which should protect all children. We run a programme of training to support these procedures. However, shortages of social workers and resources prevent the work being carried out. There are systems which work when followed appropriately but children and families do not always fit systems. Professionals working at crisis point mean that those in need do not always get the appropriate services. (LEA Officer)

Although the majority were more confident that those *at risk* would receive a more appropriate response than those *in need*, there was widespread concern that staffing pressures in key professional groups had made systems unsafe. Recent public enquiries and high profile cases were quoted as proof that systems alone cannot prevent child deaths. Despite the fact that current practice is based on a multi-agency approach the major responsibility still lies with Social Services. They determine the thresholds for action and subsequent response, which means that other agencies may find it very difficult to interpret thresholds without good channels of communication to allow explanations for action or inaction to be fed back. A number of suggestions were made for improving communication between the agencies involved, including the establishment of multi-disciplinary teams. The centralisation of services was seen as a key factor that militated against this happening:

A very positive initiative would be to link individual schools or geographical patches or pyramids of schools to particular social workers in a manner similar to the school-based social workers of several years ago. This would go towards breaking down many of the barriers between Education and Social Services, and would also help to break down some of the mistrust of social workers in some communities. Many schools and individual social workers would welcome these links, but the present resources, guidance and structures make it an impossible dream. (A Chief Education Social Worker)

Similarly, a multi-agency approach would ideally mean that other agencies, such as schools and health visitors, could take the lead in identifying services to support those *in need*, but this is often frustrated by those services requiring a referral to be made by Social Services. In addition, such services are thin on the ground, may not be known to other agencies such as schools, and these other agencies may not regard it as appropriate or feasible to undertake such a referral. Although the present system is theoretically founded on a multi-agency approach that assumes there is an equality of responsibility between services, in reality Social Services are often regarded not only as the lead agency but also the senior partner. As a consequence, sometimes it is only when there is a crisis that a cohesive multi-agency response occurs. All too often the agencies that have the potential to be part of a joined up preventative strategy are unable to trigger appropriate responses from their partners:

There are no brownie points for making multi-agency referrals for dealing with children who are challenging, until there is a scandal. Then the questions may be asked, why the agencies did not work together. (LEA Officer)

The question of how to achieve a more proactive, less reactive, response is being asked in many authorities.

Responses to older children

There was a substantial proportion of respondents who thought that students in secondary schools were likely to get a less adequate response than those in primary schools. Only a minority of respondents proffered an explanation for their opinion, although those that did suggested reasons that are worthy of further examination. Some thought it was a matter of balancing resources. If it were possible to weigh the risks and if the choice were between reacting to a six year old and a fourteen year old, the former would attract attention because they would be seen to be less able to look after themselves. There were those who also thought that the earlier an intervention took place the greater the chance of long term success and that teenagers may have experienced so much abuse that the chances of success were significantly diminished. So in terms of cost effectiveness the younger child would be seen as the better bet. Some respondents speculated about the actual age of consent in relation to sexual relationships and others debated the triggers for Social Services' intervention in the lives of teenagers:

> *Just doing things of which adults disapprove does not make it a child protection issue. If they visit houses where there is prostitution, or where drugs are circulating, Social Services are reluctant to see those things as child protection issues unless that behaviour is attributable to lack of care by the parent.* (LEA Officer)

But there were a number of references to the problems that were created for schools when no one seemed to assume responsibility. Schools may make a referral because they think the child needs protecting but they are then told that for Social Services to intervene the referral requires parental consent. When this is refused or appointments are not kept the school may feel they are left to deal with quite complex problems:

> *It may well be that parents do not want Social Services involved or they cannot be bothered. It all takes time. The child may be causing problems in school or be truanting and at further risk because of lack of supervision. This is a problem for child protection in general with older children. The procedures are based on the assumption that the child is the passive agent.* (LEA Officer)

> *We have interpreted a lot of things that happen to older children as not being attributable to abuse. We do not perceive ten year olds who kill a child as victims. At the age of ten you are responsible for your own life so why are we interfering with the lives of children over ten? There is a mixed message that small children deserve to be protected but that older children who are putting themselves at risk do not deserve protection. I have had conversations with social workers where they have said of 12 and 13 year olds, 'If that is the way they want to live who are we to say it is not appropriate?' It is a cop out. Some professionals do not want to bite the bullet. But then again a lot of responses would require co-operation and resources which are just not there.* (Chief Education Welfare Officer)

Although only a minority of respondents chose to comment on their perceptions that older children were less likely to receive a response, whether they were *at risk* or *in need*, those that did raised points which demand further investigation. The comments made point to the fact that in too many instances ACPC procedures, *Working Together* and even the *Assessment Framework* do not provide the means for dealing with the problems posed by older young people who do not want to co-operate in their own protection or whose behaviour places them *at risk* rather than necessarily any failure by their parents. This, in turn, begs the question of whether a different approach for this group of challenging young people is needed.

Education Act (2002)

Section 175 of the *Education Act* (2002) which received Royal Assent in July 2002 states:

> *(1) A local education authority shall make arrangements for ensuring that the functions conferred on them in their capacity as a local education authority are exercised with a view to safeguarding and promoting the welfare of children.*
>
> *(2) The governing body of a maintained school shall make arrangements for ensuring that their functions relating to the conduct of the school are exercised with a view to safeguarding and promoting the welfare of children who are pupils at the school.*

This section, an amendment to the *Education Bill*, appeared quickly and was rushed through Parliament before the 2002 summer adjournment. The survey had been distributed and responses returned before the amendment was known. However, the legislative change caused a great deal of concern amongst teachers and their professional representatives who feared individuals could be held accountable for a failure to recognise or report a child who was subsequently found to have been abused.[15] It seemed appropriate to attempt to collect the initial responses from LEAs on the amendment. As the summer break loomed a postal survey would have been destined to sit around in too many in-trays only to be drowned by the pressures of the autumn term. The compromise was to email the 57 respondents who had provided an email address on their contact sheet. A short email gave details of the amendment (as set out above) and then asked:

> • *Is it necessary to place this on a statutory footing?*
> • *Do you think it will make any difference to practice?*
> • *What, if anything, do you think:*
>
> *a) the LEA will have to do in response?*
> *b) schools will have to do in response? to meet this responsibility.*
>
> *I would, of course, welcome any further comments or observations on this proposed amendment.*

Forty-two respondents replied. A few admitted that they had believed there was already a statutory duty. The role of the LEA in promoting the welfare and protection of children is clearly specified in the guidance of Circular 10/95 and documents such as *Working Together* which originate in the *Children Act* (1989). Many LEA Ofsted reports already refer to whether or not the authority is meeting its statutory requirements, but are not necessarily consistent in what they judge these to be. Perhaps a statutory statement was needed to clarify the position and, of course, earlier statements had not extended the responsibility to schools.

The idea of making LEAs and schools statutorily responsible for safeguarding and promoting the welfare of children was generally welcomed by just over half of the 42 respondents,

---

[15]For example, see *The Guardian*, 29 June 2002.

although many of them were reluctant to be too positive without further details about what this would entail, what LEAs and schools would be expected to do and details of any additional resources which may be put in place to support its introduction. There were many unanswered questions, not least of which was what 'safeguarding and promoting the welfare of children' actually meant. The debates during the Bill's passage made clear reference to child protection and the impetus for the amendment had been the death of a school aged child at the hands of her step-mother, but the wording introduced the possibility of much wider interpretation. Subsequently *Safeguarding Children: A Joint Chief Inspectors' Report on Arrangements to Safeguard Children* (Department of Health, 2002) pointed out the term *safeguarding* had not been defined in law or Government guidance. Instead it had evolved from the initial concern about children and young people in public care to include the protection from harm of all children and young people and to cover all agencies working with children and their families. The Inspectors interpreted the term to mean:

> *all agencies working with children, young people and their families take all reasonable measures to ensure that the risks of harm to children's welfare are minimised;*

and

> *where there are concerns about children and young people's welfare, all agencies take all appropriate actions to address those concerns, working to agreed local policies and procedures in full partnership with other local agencies.*

Respondents who were less than enthusiastic fell into two camps. There were those who contended that if the resources had been put into place, across all agencies and not just in Education, this kind of legislation would not have been necessary. And there was a small, but not insignificant, group antagonistic to the legislation.

Although it was possible to distinguish between those that welcomed the amendment and those that did not, there was little to distinguish the accompanying remarks. Just over one third of respondents viewed it as a *knee-jerk response* and *an over reaction* to the case of Lauren Wright, the six year old who had died at the hands of her stepmother who worked in the school which she attended. Despite the fact that teachers had concerns about the child these had not been passed on to Social Services. The report into the circumstances leading to the death of Lauren in May 2000 detailed failings by both the Health Authority and Social Services. It also highlighted shortcomings in procedures by the LEA insofar as the school Lauren attended did not have a teacher trained in child protection – a breach of local-authority guidelines. But some respondents commented that this would be the case in so few schools around the country that while one answer would be to ensure a tighter monitoring of training it was doubtful that legislation was needed to do this. The implication of legislating was that Education had been identified as culpable to a greater extent than other agencies when the report had not reached that conclusion. This LEA officer summed up many of the reservations expressed by both those who welcomed it and those who did not:

> *Given the detailed DfES guidance on this for schools and the fact that Ofsted inspection criteria include the school's child protection function I think this new add-on requirement is some sort of political knee-jerk reaction. It may be the national playing out of the local problem that sees the tensions between child protection*

professionals and performance problems projected onto the child protection amateurs such as schools and other groups. It also means nothing until the detailed guidance behind it is available. It's a very general statement as it stands. Any change would best wait to fit in with the post Climbié developments. None of this is to underestimate the crucial role of schools in child welfare but given the need for working together at all times in this area I don't think changing one agency's role on its own is very productive. The most useful immediate thing that could be done to support children's welfare in schools would be provision of a ring fenced budget to pay for supply cover whilst teachers trained in child protection or attended conferences. (Senior Officer with Responsibility for Child Protection)

Most respondents, whatever their opinion, believed they already fulfil this function under Circular 10/95 by ensuring that they have a designated teacher for child protection and that training is accessed year on year through the LEA. They believed they were doing everything they were required to do without legislative compulsion and that it would make little difference to their practice. However, it was thought that in some cases an authority may find the statutory requirement increased their influence in relation to schools recalcitrant over attending training. If it became compulsory it would give child protection a higher priority than previously:

This authority is big enough for them to hide quietly in a corner. The amendment will be useful in reminding them of their now statutory duty to comply. But a far more effective tool has been the attitude of inspection teams to child safety issues. (LEA Officer)

It will give us teeth to challenge those schools who still do not follow the guidance properly. (LEA Officer)

A minority of those in favour of the amendment actually thought that the new powers might not be strong enough. Their reservations stemmed from the wording of the amendment, which was seen to be too vague and open to interpretation. This was viewed as contrary to what some saw to be one of its major advantages: it had the potential to achieve greater consistency between authorities in practice, training and support. In short, it was a way of ensuring a standard of practice. Current standards of child protection management in LEAs nationally are very much a matter of chance, depending on the level of commitment of individual officers within LEAs.

But the majority of respondents believed most schools did not need compulsion and that there were other impediments which stopped them from attending training and child protection conferences, such as cover arrangements and shortage of permanent and supply staff, which would have to be ameliorated before any significant change was possible. This response encapsulates a widespread opinion amongst the respondents:

My overriding (personal) thought re. the amendment is that, given there has been an undertaking that appropriate funding will be made available to undertake the statutory responsibility, both LEAs and schools will be able to put appropriate staff time and resources against CP responsibilities and this would make a huge difference. This does of course assume that the funding is sufficient…! My belief is that there is not a problem with hearts and minds re. protecting children in education. However there is, in some authorities, a problem with funding to both deliver training and support from the LEA and to provide school based staff with the dedicated time and supply cover to undertake their responsibilities. Budget allocation does prioritise statutory functions.… Even in my authority, where funding against CP is good relative to many other authorities we could, of course, be doing a lot more if we had more money. (Senior Officer with Responsibility for Child Protection)

However, given the difficulties experienced in recruiting supply teachers to cover for those wanting to attend training sessions even when funding was available, there may be further hurdles to negotiate.

Until the guidance and regulations that will accompany this part of the legislation are available it is difficult to know what might be expected of LEAs and schools, but respondents were asked to speculate. There was the obvious demand for clarification of what was actually meant by 'functions conferred on them in their capacity as a local education authority are exercised with a view to safeguarding and promoting the welfare of children'. There was concern that such imprecise wording could be used to launch numerous test cases against LEAs (and similarly against schools) or could result in such general interpretation as to render it meaningless.

The suggestions made by respondents are already established practice in some LEAs and schools, and the exercise was designed to tease out what would be needed to meet the requirements not only of the new legislation but also the demands of Ofsted.

What local education authorities will have to do in response

There was a high level of agreement in response to this question. Five main areas emerged which would need to be targeted by LEAs to support the work they saw as resulting from the amendment. These were:

- The review of staffing and other resources devoted to child protection in order to make an appropriate allocation to meet the standard of practice required.

- The appointment or identification of a discrete LEA child protection post where one does not exist. This response was typical:

  It will only make a difference to practice if LEAs appoint a full-time child protection officer to oversee the schools. This person could be responsible for visiting schools and checking on policies, procedures and making sure all staff are trained. However, how many LEAs would provide full-time posts unless extra funding were provided remains to be seen. (LEA Officer)

- A closer relationship between LEAs and ACPCs, possibly facilitated by the post holder suggested above.

- The means to respond to the expected demand from schools for support:

  If this does become statutory I think initially the LEA will be overrun by requests from teachers regarding advice and action, as will Social Services. Clearly the LEA will have to have a substantial training programme in place and the support function to schools would have to be re-negotiated. This will also depend on what happens following the Laming report. In [this LEA] the Education Department has its own child protection manual which compliments ACPC guidance. There is a rigorous training programme on offer to all schools and non-teaching staff. The CEWO offers professional advice and support to all Heads and CPCOS regarding the assessment and management of risk – schools already feel overstretched to deliver their responsibility – adding child protection to this will not be welcomed. This is probably not necessary if communication between agencies improves and clarification of accountability is made explicit. (LEA Officer)

- Provision of an appropriate range of training to meet the needs of all teachers and others working in schools and a regular review of attendance and record of training received by designated teachers specifically and schools in general, especially as the data in relation to training of designated teachers, support staff and newly qualified staff may be inspected.

What schools will have to do in response

- Recognise that they (i.e. all schools equally) have a key responsibility in the area of child protection.

- Plan structured training for all staff in relation to child protection.

- Access the training and support offered by the LEA.

- Appoint a nominated governor for child protection who has received appropriate training.

- Report to governors annually on the management of child protection in the school.

- Identify a member of the school's senior leadership team to be designated teacher with responsibility for child protection, even if a second designated teacher is appointed who does not hold such seniority, to allow that person the opportunity to effect change and influence attitudes.

- Allow the designated teacher sufficient time away from school to attend training, conferences and other meetings.

Although these were identified as key factors for schools to be able to meet their responsibilities there was widespread recognition of what else would be needed to ensure universal implementation. Additional resources at both LEA and school level were seen as a prerequisite. But even with adequate budgetary provision there was not a ready-made solution to finding cover for teachers to leave school to attend training and/or meetings. Similarly, appropriate and clear guidance to accompany the introduction of the Act was seen to be essential, but it was hoped that this would be drawn up after consulting with all the parties concerned, including themselves and representatives of teachers and governors.

Just over one third chose to make additional comments, all of which identified at least one of three major challenges which could threaten a more effective approach to child protection.

The first of these concerned training-related issues. There were comments about the generally low level of awareness which teachers have of child protection issues, in contrast to their commitment to the subject. The content on initial teacher training courses was seen to be superficial and too many students had failed to access what was on offer. Similarly, too little training was said to be occurring in schools with the general body of teachers and ancillary staff. It was seen to be a very big gap to be bridged but one that needed a significant shift if practice were to improve. But while LEAs hoped they could influence and support schools the second challenge was seen to be beyond their control. This was the lack of consistency in the responses received from Social Services, usually caused by staff shortages and reorganisations, which could then act as a disincentive for schools to make a referral. There was some anxiety and even irritation about the imposition of statutory responsibilities on LEAs and schools without any recognition that in order to fulfil their responsibilities they depended on the partner agencies acting appropriately.

Another concern was about the possibility of increased pressure on schools to play safe when assessing the risk one child may pose to another and use exclusion more readily. Some respondents were also worried that fewer teachers would be interested in taking on the role of designated teacher for child protection – 'because, God knows, it's onerous enough as it is' – particularly as they considered that media coverage of the passage of the amendment had served to raise teachers' anxieties and produce negative responses to the subject of child protection, which had not existed previously:

> *With regard to schools I think they will respond with irritation and… it could have the opposite effect from that which was intended. At our Summer Seminar for Heads on child protection this legislative change had just been announced and, because the headlines had been about teachers being sued if they did not report child abuse, there was a lot of anger about. I tried to turn it around, saying that we knew all our schools in this authority were committed to child protection… and that their presence at the Seminar reflected where we were at.* (Senior Officer with Responsibility for Child Protection)

Those respondents who replied towards the end of the summer of 2002 also speculated that teachers' concerns and disenchantment with the procedures may have increased over the holiday as they had watched the unfolding difficulties in relation to the failure of the Criminal Records Bureau[16] to complete the required checks on new staff:

> *The Bureau was not quite* [the] *knee-jerk that the amendment is but it was equally unthought through.* (LEA Officer)

What is needed

Respondents also had clear ideas about what they wanted to see in place as the legislation came into effect. There were many calls for the DfES to issue clear guidance written in consultation with experienced LEA and school personnel. Some respondents wanted to see a code of practice or a set of minimum standards to underpin the amendment. This was seen as a means of raising the awareness of both schools and authorities to their duties under the legislation and help monitor how they were responding. But most respondents did not think that much could be achieved within current budgets. Earmarked funding, to support training and supply costs, was seen as essential. They hoped that the resources mentioned when the draft bill was under discussion would materialise because without them they believed very little could be achieved.

---

[16] The Criminal Records Bureau (CRB) is an executive agency of the Home Office, but delays in the checking system being run by the CRB meant that many teachers had not been cleared by the beginning of the 2002-2003 school year and the Secretary of State for Education had to drop the DfES's insistence that all applicants for positions in schools had to undergo these checks before starting work.

Observations

Most respondents had faith in the present system though not to its implementation and interpretation. They were committed to a multi-agency approach which requires widespread (and possibly compulsory) training of staff in all the agencies involved if the *Assessment Framework* and *Working Together to Safeguard Children* are to be given a chance of succeeding. There is a great deal of training being carried out by LEAs but many find it difficult to ensure that all designated teachers are adequately prepared. Yet the designated teachers will be only as effective as the teachers in their schools. If those who come into contact with children and young people are confident about their responsibilities in relation to child protection and about the appropriate responses to those in their care, designated teachers are in a better position to fulfil their role. But this can only be achieved if they are adequately prepared for their role. Some respondents in LEAs expressed their concerns about the growing number of initiatives in schools, which mean many more individuals in contact with children, and the difficulties they faced in providing child protection training or even child protection awareness.

The survey has allowed LEAs the opportunity to set out the very positive work many are doing in fulfilling their responsibilities in the field of child protection, as well as identify areas which challenge them and those where their responsibility or power to act remain somewhat grey. It has also allowed them to reflect on recent developments and to express their frustrations. Sometimes these frustrations related to the additional responsibilities that had been placed upon them, when a number commented that their powers to compel schools to meet the expectations of the LEA had been severely constrained. Sometimes frustrations related to the lack of consultation before significant changes were introduced. The expertise in many LEAs, reflected in part in their assessment of what is needed to improve the effectiveness of the child protection system, should be recognised as they will play an important part in working towards a safer society for children.

Section 3: Ofsted reports on local education authorities and child protection

Since 1998 local education authority (LEA) inspections have been conducted by Her Majesty's Inspectors (HMI) from Ofsted under powers conferred on Her Majesty's Chief Inspector of Schools by Section 38 of the *Education Act* (1997).[17] The principal purpose of the inspections is to review the way LEAs perform their functions in support of school improvement, special educational provision, access and strategic management. The remit is wide and does involve discussions with other departments of the authority, but the major focus of these inspections is the LEA. Although it is important to recognise that LEAs are also subject to other inspection and audit processes, they do not always seem to take full account of their perspectives, as one respondent to the survey reported in Section 1 described:

> *A recent Social Services Inspectorate inspection of child protection included an educational perspective but based on a half-hour interview shared with Health! That put us in our place.* (LEA Officer)

Inspections of local education authorities are carried out in conjunction with the Audit Commission and follow a framework, which serves as a guide for both the LEA and HMI. Since February 2002 Ofsted and Audit Commission inspectors have been using the guidance set out in *Framework for the Inspection of Local Education Authorities* (Her Majesty's Chief Inspector of Schools in England, 2002) when undertaking organisational inspections of LEAs. All LEAs have been inspected at least once, and the *Framework* is said to draw upon lessons learnt since the start of LEA inspections in 1998. The stated principle underlying these inspections is that Ofsted 'will be testing to see whether, more widely, LEAs have moved on in their vital role of supporting schools in raising standards for all children and supporting social inclusion'.

One hundred and forty Ofsted reports were examined[18] to see what they said about the ways in which they were meeting their responsibilities in relation to child protection. These reports referred to inspections completed between 1999 and 2002 so the majority were conducted under the original *Framework*. In 1999, of the 37 reports examined, six contained no reference to child protection, but this fell to only one of the 49 reports examined from the year 2000 and

---

[17] Education in Wales is run by the Welsh Assembly. It is responsible for setting the principality's education strategy as well as distributing budgets and controlling the quangos that oversee schools, further education colleges and universities. There is a separate Welsh Inspectorate, Estyn. Estyn carries out inspections of local education authorities under Section 38 of the *Education Act* (1997). This gives the Chief Inspector the power to arrange for any local education authority (LEA) to be inspected. It also requires Estyn to inspect any LEA if asked to do so by the Welsh Assembly Government. The Department of Education Northern Ireland (DENI) engages its own Education and Training Inspectorate (ETI) to carry out inspections. The inspection reports for Wales and Northern Ireland were not examined.

[18] These were accessed through the Ofsted website www.ofsted.gov.uk

there were no such omissions in subsequent years. These seven reports are omitted from the figures presented below, because they make no reference to child protection; the analysis is therefore based on the 133 reports that did. As all reports completed in 2001 and subsequently dealt with child protection, and in light of the revised *Framework* it seems unlikely that such an omission will occur in the future.

Four major areas were identified for the analysis. These are:

• Procedures put in place by the LEA in relation to child protection

• The extent to which an LEA is meeting its statutory responsibilities

• The relationship which an LEA has with the Social Services department

• The training which the LEA supports on child protection.

Procedures

Of the 133 reports examined 79 per cent (105) commented on the procedures the LEA had established in relation to child protection. Over the years the proportion of reports not referring to procedures has declined. So while a third of the 1999 reports failed to address this aspect, this fell to just over a quarter of the 2000 reports, and one tenth of those written in 2001. All of the 2002 reports examined covered the procedures that were in place. Most of the comments were positive, although there was a lack of consistency in the way this was approached. In some cases there was a very cursory reference to aspects of the procedures:

> *Documentary evidence and guidance on child protection are sound.*

> *Clear procedures have been revised and an information booklet provided for teachers and other adults.*

> *Good support and guidance.*

Although there were a number of exceptions, the later reports tended to contain more detailed references, taking a broader view of the issue and an LEA's response, as the following extracts illustrate:

> *Procedures are very good. The LEA has a well-developed strategy that runs through its plans and services based on a detailed analysis of need. The authority gives a strong lead on child protection and has been identified by the DfES as a lead for a cluster of authorities [in the area].*

> *Procedures for child protection are good. The creation of the post of child protection adviser in the mid-90s was welcomed by Social Services and is viewed by officers and staff in schools as having been influential in taking forward co-ordinated action to protect children. The revised child protection policy and procedures are robust and are ready to be presented to elected members. The document sets out clearly the role of the LEA and its partners. It provides a framework to encourage consistency of policies and practice within the county and a context for establishing good practice for the protection of children.*

And not all the observations were on exemplary practice:

> *The child protection procedures are unsatisfactory, but the weaknesses which have been identified are being addressed and improvement has taken place over the last six months. The procedures and support for protecting children from significant harm have improved recently but remain unsatisfactory in two key ways....*

That report goes on to indicate how the LEA needs to promote training of teachers and develop appropriate routes for communication between schools and social workers, but it also commends aspects of the newly drawn up guidelines, indicating areas where they could be strengthened. Such an approach contributes to the development of good practice and indicates how the process of inspection can help the development of a multi-agency response to the welfare of children. Some reports acknowledged the effect that working with other bodies may have on a LEA's effectiveness. Sometimes the effects can be positive as in the first example below, but they can also jeopardise the LEA's ability to perform its responsibilities effectively as in the second instance. Both LEAs are part of unitary authorities which came into existence less than five years previously and have had to separate themselves from the originating authorities and establish their own ways of working:

> *The arrangements for child protection are satisfactory, the strengths outweigh weaknesses and there are clear signs of improvement. Following a Social Services inspection two years ago, Social Services has vigorously tackled the issues raised and the problems identified. Inherited procedures for handling child protection issues have been revised in line with the Framework for Assessment.*

> *At local government re-organisation the council adopted the originating authority's child protection procedures. So the ACPC did not come into existence until April 1999. A revised and comprehensive handbook dealing with child protection procedures has been issued to schools. Arrangements to develop a child protection policy for the LEA's schools have been slow and are still in their infancy. This is due primarily to a lack of consensus among ACPC representatives as to whether the six unitary authorities should work together on joint policies and procedures or each council develop their own.*

Statutory responsibilities

Only 41 per cent of the inspection reports actually referred to whether the LEA was meeting its statutory responsibilities. Once again the proportion containing such a reference increased over the years until 2002, although not as significantly as in relation to procedures. But as only nine reports were available for 2002 that trend should be re-examined once a complete set of reports is available. The fact that there is a large proportion of reports where this is not dealt with may reflect the fact that there is an assumed overlap with procedures, which received more widespread comment. However, in 15 per cent of the reports no reference was made to the LEA's procedures for child protection or to how it was fulfilling its statutory responsibilities, although with only a few exceptions these were inspections that occurred prior to 2001.

It may also be that the issue would be dealt with only if the LEA were blatantly not fulfilling its statutory responsibilities. None of the reports contained a specific reference to an authority that was not meeting its responsibilities, although one report commented:

Apart from concerns regarding the monitoring of pupils' removal from registers the LEA meets statutory requirements in relation to child protection and welfare.

There were very few references to this specific aspect of monitoring, so it is hard to know if other inspections did not address the issue or if it was not referred to in reports. From many discussions with teachers and representatives of LEAs around the country it is not something which is routinely undertaken by LEAs and depends heavily on information received from Social Services and schools. If schools do not attend case reviews and if communication with Social Services is less effective than it should be, there may be a period of time when they are unaware that a child is no longer on the child protection register. *Safeguarding Children: A Joint Chief Inspectors' Report on Arrangements for Safeguarding Children* (Department of Health, 2002) commented on the confusion they had found in agencies over responsibilities and duties to share information about child welfare concerns with other agencies, and were not confident about whether other agencies shared information with them. It refers to the findings of inquiries over past years where there had been serious weaknesses and failings in information sharing, but the inspectors had found very few formal agreements between agencies about how and when information should be shared.

Throughout the reading of the Ofsted reports there were numerous examples of single issues taken as indicators of success or failure in specific LEAs that did not appear in other reports. However, with the new *Framework* it may be that greater consistency and a sharper focus will be achieved.

Relationship with Social Services

In just over half (53 per cent) the reports examined reference was made to the relationship between the LEA and Social Services at a strategic level and/or as part of a multi-agency approach to child protection. Only a minority of reports produced in 1999 and 2000 contained such a reference while the majority of the 2001 reports did. The trend continued in the 2002 reports examined. This may reflect a more rigorous approach to inspections but may also be a result of *Working Together to Safeguard Children* (1999) which strengthened the multi-agency approach to protection.

The majority of these references were to good or at least satisfactory practice. Once again there was a range of responses covering working relationships on ACPCs, the structures in place at managerial level to co-ordinate work across the departments, strategic partnerships, joint working arrangements and joint protocols in relation to speed of referrals and other issues. It would be useful to have a clearer definition of what indicators should be used to assess the relationship between these two agencies.

Although there were some comments about how the relationship could be improved and strengthened the general impression from the reports which covered it was one where LEAs were assuming an active role within the multi-agency framework. However, the picture was less rosy when the views of schools on their relationship with Social Services are taken into account. This difference was also detected by the Inspectors from the different agencies who undertook the joint inspection on arrangements for safeguarding children (Department of Health, 2002) who commented:

Relationships between senior Social Services and education staff, particularly within the Local Education Authority, were normally better than those between Social Services and school staff. Relationships between school staff and Social Services were sometimes unduly influenced by past experiences and personal contacts.

Just over a quarter of the reports analysed contained a reference to schools' views on their relationship with Social Services in relation to child protection. With a few notable exceptions most of the feedback from schools was that this liaison was either unsatisfactory or in need of significant improvement. Of the 37 reports containing any reference to schools' views on this relationship only two were exclusively positive, although in four reports schools were said to have different experiences depending on the relationships with local teams and individuals:

Liaison between the LEA and relevant Social Services and health agencies is good at a strategic level. The quality of day-to-day dealings with Social Services personnel at school and local office level is more dependent on the efforts of individuals than robust systems.

Most of the criticism focused on concerns about delayed responses to pupil referrals and to the failure of Social Services to provide feedback on progress of cases or timely information:

In the survey 57 per cent of primary schools and all secondary schools judged the effectiveness of liaison with Social Services to be unsatisfactory or worse. Communication between education and Social Services is not always effective at school level owing to frequent changes in Social Services personnel. During the inspection schools raised concerns about recent, conflicting advice from within Social Services about referral procedures.

Attempts to improve relationships between schools and Social Services through presentations at head teachers' meetings and through allocating named social workers to schools, have only been partly implemented. Relationships between schools and Social Services vary and are too dependent upon the individuals concerned. The point at which Social Services intervene on behalf of individual children is not always clear to teachers, and there is no rigorously implemented system of feedback on specific cases.

In some cases a report acknowledged the efforts of LEAs in attempting to improve the situation. However, it was apparent that in many areas – while communication was rated as being good at senior levels and where efforts had been made to develop strong strategic partnerships – this did not always translate to practice on the ground, as these examples illustrate:

The LEA makes an appropriate contribution to the work of the ACPC. There has been good collaboration between the LEA, Social Services... to develop child protection procedures. But liaison between education and Social Services is unsatisfactory at the school level. In response to previous criticism there is now a named contact within Social Services for each secondary school and this has improved day to day communications for these schools. Schools still cite examples of poor response regarding children potentially at risk. The LEA should investigate these cases to identify gaps in provision. Alternatively where schools have unrealistic expectations of Social Services, there is currently no guidance on referral to other relevant services.

The LEA plays a full part in the ACPC. Communication between services is good at the senior level and every effort is being made to develop strong structures locally, with a named social worker for every school, and an interdisciplinary monitoring group based on every pyramid of schools. Occasionally the initial advice a school received was less than authoritative or it was difficult to access a social worker quickly. The difficulty is that, as elsewhere in the country, there are shortages of social workers in some areas. The situation will continue to need close monitoring by the partners and is a factor to bear in mind in any proposals for restructuring the education welfare service.

In some instances the authorities had been through previous inspections where weaknesses had been identified. Although this analysis dealt with full reports it is interesting to look at particular examples of authorities where full inspections were followed by short inspections to monitor progress. In one authority, which was judged to be failing, a contractor had been appointed to strengthen key areas of the LEA's services. In the 1999 inspection the procedures and support for child protection were satisfactory, problems of liaison between education and Social Services, at both authority and school level, were commented upon. By 2001 the current arrangements for protecting children from significant harm were said to be unsatisfactory. The authority continued to go through re-organisation and restructuring that were bringing their own challenges. Providing a service for child protection was originally specified as a direct responsibility of the LEA. However, varying the contract to place responsibility directly with the contractor was put forward for consideration, alongside other specific recommendations:

- *decide whether variations are required in the contract regarding responsibility for providing a child protection service, clarify the member of staff at a senior level who will act as the nominated lead officer, and collaborate with Social Services to devise strategies for promoting better working arrangements between social workers and schools;*

- *in collaboration with the ACPC, devise supplementary guidance to schools which provides them with detailed information about how they should discharge their responsibilities for protecting children;*

- *keep an up-to-date list of schools' designated teachers with the dates of their most recent training; and*

- *in consultation with head teachers, devise and adopt a suitable training policy to ensure that schools have a member of staff confident in managing the requirements of the school's child protection policy.*

While all these may be sensible suggestions as part of a strategy for improvement, they fail to address directly the concerns expressed by schools – difficulties in establishing effective communication with, and receiving a response and support from, Social Workers when there were children they considered to be at risk. The report does acknowledge that senior staff in the Social Services department recognise that there is much to be done to establish effective joint working with Education, and that change will be effected only when it moves beyond the strategic level and has an impact on practice. The difficulty of effecting such change should not be underestimated, especially as it depends on actions beyond the control of LEAs. Not only does it require schools to act appropriately, it must then trigger a response from Social Services, which accepts the referral or communicates the reasons for alternative action or inaction.

However, it is becoming evident that Ofsted will judge LEAs accountable for effecting improvements at an operational level. This is well illustrated by focusing on inspections in three authorities.

Despite the anxieties expressed by schools about responses from social workers to their concerns about child protection matters, an earlier inspection of one LEA judged links with Social Services on child protection to be good. However, the number and nature of the weaknesses identified led to the conclusion that the LEA was not succeeding in promoting high standards in schools. The inspection also questioned the ability of the LEA to provide the 'strong and sustained educational leadership that its schools needed'.

The re-inspection, less than two years later, concluded that the LEA had made substantial progress in a very short time. It was said to perform 'the great majority of its functions satisfactorily; strengths now heavily outweigh weaknesses which, although few, are significant'. However, its child protection arrangements were said to be unsatisfactory. It recognised that the LEA was taking reasonable steps to meet its statutory responsibilities at a strategic level but that this was not being reflected at school level. The difference between the two reports also reflects a shift in Ofsted thinking in the intervening period. It is no longer enough to have established good links at management level. These have to be transmitted to practice and withstand the evaluation of schools. Schools still judged as inadequate the response from Social Services to the concerns they raised. Although senior managers in Education and Social Services were aware of the concerns, and had worked together to establish a shared strategy to address them, insufficient progress was judged to have been made. The report contained a specific recommendation that the LEA had to tackle schools' concerns about the effectiveness of communication with Social Services in order to build trust in child protection arrangements. This hinges on the co-operation of two distinct agencies which, while they may share common goals, have distinct staff groupings, budgets and even cultures. All of which would have to be addressed if a truly multi-agency approach is to stand a chance of success.

In another authority a full inspection was conducted in 1999, and a short inspection in 2001 followed up the progress of the LEA in implementing the post-inspection action plan and its Education Development Plan. In 1999 the inspection identified sound liaison between the LEA and Social Services Directorate at senior levels but schools expressed frustration with social workers, especially when they were not informed about any action taken regarding children they judged to be *at risk*. The recommendation was that day-to-day communication between schools and social workers should be strengthened. The second report goes on to say:

> *This has happened. Performance and progress are satisfactory with few weaknesses. The Social Services department has reorganised its service so that each of its relevant teams is linked to one of the pyramids of schools and SSD, health and education boundaries are now coterminous. There has been joint training of representatives of the different agencies and work on the Assessment Framework has led to improvement in this area, especially through the two pilots on the Framework. There are new protocols about the rates of response to referrals. Discussions with head teachers indicated that in secondary schools the position remains patchy but in pilot areas and among primary schools generally there has been a significant improvement.*

Obviously these improvements have not come about only through the efforts of the LEA or as a result of the previous Ofsted inspection, but the report and its recommendations will have played a role in focusing attention on the appropriate response to bring about improvement.

In the final authority far more serious problems existed. Child protection had not been identified as an area of weakness in the first report, although the LEA was judged to have severe weaknesses. In the two years between the two inspections it was said that insufficient progress had been made. In the spring of 2001 the then Secretary of State for Education and Skills had directed the appointment of an outside consultant as a strategic partner 'to build the capacity for providing effective support to schools'. It was acknowledged that the Education department had played a key role in the recent development of a newly formed ACPC that intended to assume responsibility for child protection policies, procedures and training across all agencies. The second report also acknowledged that identified weaknesses were being addressed and improvements had taken place. However, while it recognised that the LEA's procedures and support for protecting children from significant harm had shown some improvement, the LEA was still judged to be unsatisfactory in a number of ways, one of which was in developing effective communication between schools and social workers. So although the Directors of both services were meeting regularly and strategic liaison was said to be improving, this was not having an impact on liaison between schools and social workers. The report then went on to make very specific recommendations aimed at improving what was obviously a major impediment to effective practice:

> *In discussion with head teachers and social workers identify the issues which require improvement in the liaison between social workers and teachers, identify ways in which they can be improved, develop greater opportunities for head teachers and social workers to discuss progress jointly and devise ways of monitoring and evaluating whether improvements are taking place.*

The more proactive nature of the new *Framework* for these inspections holds the hope that by identifying issues and making recommendations the agencies will be compelled to work together to address the sources of concern.

Training

Seventy-one per cent of the reports examined contained a reference to training provided by LEAs for teachers. Although the proportion of reports containing such a reference showed a marked increase between 1999 and 2000, over a quarter of the reports produced in 2001 made no mention of training. However, there was a perceptible shift in the quality of the information recorded about training, although there was little consistency and it was not universal. So, for example, only seven of the 31 reports in 1999 referred to LEAs keeping records of the training designated teachers had received and, sometimes by default and sometimes explicitly, of the proportion of designated teachers who had been trained.

This did become more common over the years. So in the 48 reports examined that had been written in 2000 ten contained a reference to training records, as did half of the 45 reports examined for 2001. Similarly, more attention was paid to the extent to which LEAs followed up those schools where a member of staff had not attended recent training and targeted specific schools that had not accessed any training, although this appeared in only a third of the 2001 reports. Not only is it important that newly appointed designated teachers are appropriately trained, those who have been in post for some time also need to attend training. They need to be made aware of how national and local initiatives impact on child protection procedures, as well as having the opportunity to meet and talk with colleagues. The role of Ofsted in this process provides an opportunity for good practice to be commended and disseminated and for recommendations to appear about the importance of monitoring and targeting training in a regular and consistent manner:

> *The LEA plays a full role in multi-agency training. Training is generally well-regarded by schools and attendance is monitored and cross-referenced to the designated teacher list. The LEA monitors child protection referrals from schools and Ofsted reports. This enables the LEA to target training for individual schools to supplement the three-year rolling programme. The follow-up of non-attendance at training by individual schools is less secure.*

> *The LEA cannot systematically identify the level of training that designated teachers in each school have received. This is a weakness.*

> *A register of designated teachers and their training is maintained. Training by the LEA has been provided in those cases where Social Services, because of staffing shortages, has found it difficult to support joint training. Planning is in place to improve to 71 per cent the number of designated teachers who have received training in the last four years.*

Overall there were very few references to training in relation to the *Assessment Framework*. This was intended to be a multi-agency tool and, while it may be realistic to see Social Services as the lead agency, its success will depend on all those working in other agencies having a good understanding of the rationale which underpins it and how it is put into operation. It would be unfair to castigate LEAs for failing to take a more active role in training, but it would be useful to identify the extent to which training has happened and the factors that may have impeded it.

Diminished role, increasing obligations

LEAs have been in a state of constant change since their creation in 1902, but the pace of change over the past 20 years has been unparalleled, as have the challenges they have faced. During this time their powers have been reduced as schools have been given more autonomy. In the late 1980s many predicted that LEAs would cease to exist. Schools were encouraged to opt out of local authority control, but the majority chose not to go down that route. Some ten years later they were brought back within LEA control, although it had been considerably reduced. Throughout this period LEAs had been left with certain core functions, the implementation of which sometimes seemed to be challenged by the devolution of an increasing proportion of the education budget to schools.

The role of local education authorities is still under discussion, but at the same time they are central to their areas. They are part of local government, playing a major role in delivering a range of strategies designed to meet the Government's agenda. Raising standards was added to their duties in 1998 and the Government clearly viewed this as their primary raison d'être, alongside the task of supporting social inclusion.

The Office for Standards in Education (Ofsted) and the Audit Commission reported on the findings of inspections of 91 of the 150 English local education authorities and re-inspections of ten of them. The report, *Local Education Authority Support for School Improvement* (Audit

Commission for Local Authorities in England and Wales et al., 2001) found that most LEAs perform the majority of their functions adequately. It claimed that some were 'impressive' and that some of those inspected more than once had made 'startling' progress. However, a larger number were judged to be performing unsatisfactorily – 'impeded not only by incompetence, but by the uncertainty and poor performance arising from excessive changes in Government initiatives over a number of years'. It went on to say that LEAs must 'submit themselves to market disciplines', retaining only a core of highly-paid professionals, and offering only services that schools wanted to buy. This role may allow them to maintain a monitoring role in relation to child protection but it will not necessarily enable them to give schools the support they seek (see Baginsky, forthcoming). Perhaps that is the heart of the dilemma. Ofsted introduced statutory inspections of all local authorities in England as part of the thrust to raise school standards. They are another way of exerting indirect pressure on schools. In relation to child protection it would seem more appropriate to offer support and advice. The role of LEAs in monitoring schools' compliance, alongside the increased emphasis on their statutory responsibility for safeguarding children, may mean schools feel pressure rather than support. It is also difficult to see how they will then be able to meet the obligations imposed on them by Section 175 of the *Education Act* (2002) or by Ofsted, let alone be part of a strategic approach to meet the recommendations contained in this report.

Section 4: Reflection

The definitions of *in need* and *in need of protection* and the framework for the current child protection procedures originate in the *Children Act* (1989). *Messages from Research* (Department of Health, 1995) indicated that too many children were failing to receive the support they needed because the emphasis was on investigation and child protection procedures. Resources were concentrated on the investigation and tied to assessment. This worked to the detriment of those defined as *in need,* even though many children *in need of protection* were also being denied access to the services they needed. While some authorities have been more proactive than others in adopting the re-focusing agenda, a great deal remains to be achieved. *The Children Act Now: Messages from Research* (Department of Health, 2001) confirms what the respondents to the survey reported in Section 2 believed and what the Social Services Inspectorate inspection of family-support services in 1999 concluded (Social Services Inspectorate, 1999): there are many children still in need of services not being provided. However, the same report refers to a study by Aldgate and Tunstill (1995) showing that although children's problems often came to light in school, children tended to be referred to Social Services only when there was a child protection concern. It had not been determined if this was because of Social Services' 'gate-keeping policy' or schools dealing with welfare issues within their own resources. The responses from LEAs would suggest that there may be low expectations as far as getting appropriate services for children *in need* are concerned, which may result in a self-fulfilling prophecy. *The Children Act Now: Messages from Research* also highlights a major problem in developing a more integrated, multi-agency strategy when different agencies fail to reach a common perception and definition of a problem. This is the case when definitions are moulded by agencies' priorities.

The extent to which children's services are struggling to survive under the current level of resourcing emerged in a survey conducted by the Local Government Association and the Association of Directors of Social Services in January 2002.[19] The result is the rigorous gate-keeping of services and raised thresholds for access. The consequence is that children whom schools believe to be *in need*, and whom they refer to Social Services, still often fail to reach the threshold for an intervention. Similarly, while it is good that inspections identify and recommend, and legislation compels, so much depends on the active support not just of senior managers in Social Services but on overworked and understaffed social-work teams. *Safeguarding Children: A Joint Chief Inspectors' Report on Arrangements to Safeguard Children* (Department of Health, 2002) concluded that a lack of resources is threatening efforts to safeguard children. The majority of respondents to the NSPCC survey thought that the present system would be more effective in protecting children if the pressures on staff in key professional groups were eased and if services were really re-focused to take full account of children *in need* and children of secondary school age.

In addition to these major obstacles may be added the failure of all agencies to give the same high priority to *Working Together to Safeguard Children* (Department of Health et al., 1999). It is the key document that sets out a strategy for inter-agency work to safeguard and promote the

---

[19] For a summary of the results of this survey see www.adss.org.uk

welfare of children. It was issued under Section 7 of the *Local Authority Social Services Act* (1970), which requires local authorities in their Social Services functions to act under the general guidance of the Secretary of State. As such it does not have the full force of statute, although it is expected that it will be complied with 'unless local circumstances indicate exceptional reasons which justify a variation'. It is not clear if all the Departments which collaborated over the production of *Working Together* shared this understanding of its quasi-legal status. While Social Services departments will be aware of its implications for practice the then Department for Education and Employment did not issue any guidance or briefing to LEAs or schools. While the Department may have been responding to schools' requests to reduce the amount of paperwork they received this omission may have contributed to a lower level of awareness about the implications of *Working Together* than is needed for effective co-operation between agencies. In the survey of LEAs 78 per cent claimed to have taken account of this document in the child protection training they offer, but it is not known how many of their schools have attended training since its publication. Similarly, there was no guidance for LEAs (or schools) on the *Framework for the Assessment of Children and their Families*. According to some respondents to the survey, the failure to include partner agencies in the briefings and related training for trainers led to an over-reliance on Social Services, which not only contradicted the spirit of the document but jeopardised its effective implementation.

Despite the emphasis placed on child protection requiring an inter-agency approach, in reality the responsibility mainly falls to Social Services. The situation would be improved if all partners could be expected to have a shared understanding of current practice in relation to child protection. When the statutory requirements, introduced by the *Education Act* (2002), come into operation the DfES will be required to issue guidance to schools and LEAs. It is hoped that this will not only embrace some, if not all, of the suggestions made by those who commented on the Act, but will reinforce a commitment to the principles of *Working Together* and the *Framework for the Assessment of Children and their Families.*

While many LEAs commit considerable resources and time to meeting their responsibilities in this area, the picture is not consistent. This is particularly apparent in relation to independent schools. Although they are not the direct responsibility of LEAs many are providing training and support. But it is too important to be left to chance. *Working Together* (1999) makes it clear that the position of independent schools in relation to child protection is the same as that of any other school and goes on to say:

> *It is particularly important that independent schools (including independent special schools) establish channels of communication with local Social Services departments and ACPCs, building on existing links with the local education authority, so that children requiring support receive prompt attention and any allegations of abuse can be properly investigated.*

Although there are more links between independent schools and LEAs there is still a long way to go. The report from the Inspectors of the main agencies (Department of Health, 2002) concluded that some independent schools were not well integrated into local safeguarding arrangements. Is it then the responsibility of ACPCs and, by dint of their role on ACPCs, LEAs to identify those that are not well integrated and work with them to address the problem? If that is not their role whose responsibility is it? The implementation of Section 157 of the *Education Act* (2002) will mean that independent schools will have to meet prescribed standards in relation to a range of areas including the welfare and safety of pupils. The DfES is about to consult on the statutory regulations relating to these standards. This is an important step towards achieving consistency in the arrangements for child protection across all schools.

Even where a commitment exists to the safeguarding of children the role of the other agencies is marginalised when it is Social Services that is responsible for investigating referrals and any subsequent action. The establishment of an agency for children and families, coterminous with local-authority and Health boundaries, would not only bring together all local-authority departments concerned with children and their families, but also involve other services with responsibilities for children. The Government has announced the establishment of Children's Trusts to oversee childcare. In some authorities steps have already been taken to achieve the integration of key services but more evaluation is required to assess the extent to which administrative merger is having an impact on the ground.

Greater co-ordination could also be achieved through ACPCs. ACPCs are strategically placed to safeguard children but the *Children Act* (1989) does not include a legal obligation on local authorities to establish an ACPC. *Working Together to Safeguard Children* requires local authorities to make sure that there is an ACPC covering their area, which brings together the main agencies and professionals responsible for helping to protect children from abuse and neglect. Yet the report from the Inspectors of the major agencies (Department of Health, 2002) found that in the majority of areas ACPCs were weak organisations which failed to exercise effective leadership. This is despite the fact that they are the main bodies for co-ordinating child protection across authorities and are at the centre of numerous recommendations.

In order to overcome any ambiguity over the status of ACPCs they should now be placed on a statutory footing. NSPCC and many others have called for an amendment to the *Children Act* (1989), which would place a statutory duty on agencies to be represented on their ACPCs. At the present time ACPCs depend too heavily on the voluntary commitment of agencies. One respondent to the survey wrote:

> *ACPCs would benefit from an effective budget and the employment of an independent chair. It is too important a job to be left to already overstretched individuals.*

All the evidence points to the importance of training. It is good that Ofsted is now taking a more proactive role in identifying good practice in the provision and monitoring of training when it conducts inspections in LEAs. LEAs are ideally placed to support the range of training needed for all those working in schools but, given the pressures on LEAs to meet their existing training commitments and the increasing number of non-teaching staff working in schools, it is difficult to envisage how they will be able to provide it all. However, it would be realistic to assume that they could take a facilitating role in this, either through the ACPC or otherwise. As far as teachers are concerned there is no standard requirement within their initial or ongoing professional training in relation to child protection issues. By placing ACPCs on a statutory basis training needs could be prioritised, identified and co-ordinated in a multi-agency way. A minimum standard could then be expected of the different professions that are brought together in the expectation that there is a shared understanding of the issues.

But equally as important as ACPCs in relation to schools and child protection is the role of the LEA. The context within which LEAs operate cannot be separated from the functions they are expected to fulfil. The failure of a small number of authorities, combined with Government policies that marginalised LEAs, produced a culture which devalued the work they did and placed a question mark over their future. The immediate result was to reduce the strategic role that had developed over the previous decades.

This uncertainty will continue until the Government gives a firm commitment to the survival of LEAs and clarifies the role they will play. In recent years, although the Government continues to support the greater autonomy and accountability of schools, LEAs have become an important agency for delivering new Government initiatives on raising educational standards and supporting social inclusion. A high proportion of school staff and governors interviewed by Derrington (2000) believed all schools needed LEAs to help them improve. Her evidence suggests that LEA officers and advisers provide more support to schools than is acknowledged. She also found that there was a perceived contradiction between funding arrangements and LEAs' statutory duties, which is reflected in LEAs' ability to support schools in relation to child protection.

The amendment, which was absorbed into the *Education Act* (2002) at a very late stage, places a statutory responsibility on LEAs for 'safeguarding and promoting the welfare of children'. Until the guidelines appear respondents are unsure about what will be expected of them. Although not all of them welcomed the legislation wholeheartedly the responses recorded above indicate a strong commitment to child protection. This commitment is also reflected in the ratings given by schools to their LEAs. Schools rate their local education authorities as satisfactory or better in 75 per cent of the aspects surveyed by the Audit Commission (2001) and child protection was one of the most positively rated areas.

The passage of the amendment was accompanied by media reports that built on, and heightened, the concerns of teachers that they could be held personally responsible. Although it has been specifically stated that the clause will not give rise to private actions by individuals against an authority, school or FE institution, failure by a head teacher or a member of staff to act in accordance with arrangements could lead to disciplinary or competence procedures being taken against them. Given the imprecision and breadth of the wording of the amendment there is the danger that this could become a lawyers' playground. Although respondents from LEAs were concerned to see robust guidance accompany the introduction of the new Act, and had many suggestions as to what should be included, this may not be a solution. In May 2002 a case heard in the Court of Appeal in relation to exclusions from schools[20] ruled that Circulars and the like are only guidance and are not law, direction or rules. So while schools were told they should 'have regard' to guidance, it does not have to be strictly adhered to. The assumption has to be that any guidance accompanying the 2002 Act will not be regarded as law. This in turn begs the questions of what this will mean, what can be done if the guidance is not followed and who, in the end, is responsible.

Perhaps the amendment will introduce a degree of standardisation that has not previously been present. Although the new Ofsted inspection framework does adopt a more prescriptive approach it probably could not achieve this alone. The present standards of child protection management in LEAs nationally are very much a matter of chance, depending on the level of commitment of individual officers within LEAs. Placing LEAs' responsibilities on a statutory footing may enable minimum standards within educational settings to be set nationally in order to achieve consistent practice. If the amendment to the *Education Act* (2002) achieves this it will

---

[20] S and others v. London Borough of Brent, May 2002.

be generally welcomed, despite the fact that many will continue to view it as a reaction to particular circumstances rather than reflecting a planned approach to child protection.

However, there is one piece missing from the jigsaw. LEAs do not run schools. The powers of LEAs in relation to schools have been curtailed since the introduction of local management of schools in the late 1980s. School governing bodies have all the power and the responsibility for the management, running and policy making in schools. LEAs have a strictly 'supportive and advisory' role with schools. As one respondent commented:

> *In reality, most schools rely very heavily on our support, but for those schools who would rather not have much to do with us, for whatever reason, it is very difficult to get a toehold since we have no statutory rights to compel schools to do anything. For example, we can offer child protection training for designated teachers and we can send out reminders and chide schools when staff don't attend but we have no way to compel them to attend. This is a major weakness in my view. Having said all of that, there is an expectation that LEAs will ensure that schools run properly. I guess you could say we have the responsibility without having any power.*

Most schools will work with their LEAs but the fact is that they do not have to. Maybe the statutory requirement now enacted for schools and LEAs will bring them even closer together. However, schools will also be able to look elsewhere for support while LEAs' performance will be judged by schools accessing training and having the appropriate policies and procedures in place.

This revised Framework for the inspection of LEAs forms the basis of continued LEA inspections by Ofsted and the Audit Commission from January 2002. It is evident from the reports inspected that the process is becoming more focused. In relation to child protection, inspections are becoming more consistent and increasingly auditing practice, although not to the extent that may be required once LEAs have statutory responsibility. If the new legislation is used as a stick with which to beat LEAs it will be regrettable. Harris (2001) examined a successful school–improvement project and explored the LEA's role as change agent. His conclusion was that the success of the LEA in school improvement depends on the relationship LEA advisers have with schools and the encouragement and support they provide during the process of change. He sees this as being threatened by Government policies requiring LEAs to set targets, monitor performance and intervene in schools that are failing. This is a model, Harris suggests, that produces 'school improvement through surveillance, with LEAs having less regular engagement or involvement with schools'. Nevertheless, if the revised Ofsted Framework, combined with the provisions of the Education Act (2002), is used to work towards a consistent approach from LEAs to their responsibilities it will be welcomed. But this implies a recognition of existing good practice, a commitment to its dissemination and an acknowledgement that LEAs are just one agency amongst many, where practice may be constrained or impeded by the other partners. However, if it is used to castigate individual authorities, and individual schools and teachers, the progress towards the establishment of systems which protect all children will have been set back.

Section 5: Recommendations

- **The DfES should produce clear and unambiguous guidance on the responsibilities imposed on LEAs and schools by Section 175 of the *Education Act* (2002).** LEAs have provided very useful guidance on what needs to be in place to support the introduction of this legislation and it is hoped that due attention is paid to it. Consideration should also be given to the involvement of Ofsted and other interested agencies in this process.

- **A national child protection training strategy is needed for all those working in schools in any capacity.** Training of all concerned is too important to be left to the lottery of local circumstances. It requires a strategy accompanied by resources allowing earmarked funding for a range of courses to meet the needs of workers with a wide range of backgrounds. LEAs should identify training needs more precisely. They should devise and publish, in association with the Area Child Protection Committee, an appropriate training strategy for Education and school staff, which makes use of both single and multi-agency training to develop a firmer foundation of good working procedures specifically between social workers and teachers.

- **LEAs should make their materials in relation to child protection available on their websites.** The majority of LEAs produce guidance for schools in relation to child protection but very few have published it in this way. Available in this form it would be accessible to a wider audience.

- **LEAs should attempt to facilitate the means by which schools are represented on ACPCs** and their subgroups, and encourage channels of communication to be developed to allow representatives to feed back to their colleagues.

- **Clear guidance is needed from the DfES and/or Department of Health in relation to independent schools and child protection, which sets out their responsibilities and where they may obtain support. These Departments should also clarify the responsibilities of ACPCs and LEAs in relation to these schools.** The implementation of Section 157 of the *Education Act* (2002), which will allow the Secretary of State to prescribe standards that all independent schools will have to meet in a range of areas including the welfare, health and safety of pupils is a welcome development and should support the realisation of this recommendation.

- **It is important that ACPCs raise their profile in relation to independent schools.**

- **The results of audits to determine if children's needs are being well met should be used to evaluate the system.** Some ACPCs are conducting audits where the Section 17 route is taken when a case is borderline Section 47; others are auditing the response to all children *at risk* and children *in need* referrals.

- **All LEAs should have a senior post dedicated to child protection** and these post holders should represent their LEAs on ACPCs, even if there are other representatives.

- **LEAs should take responsibility for the development and dissemination of child** protection policies for work placements and all other settings that may be used by their pupils and students.

- **Central Government should give a commitment to provide the necessary training to accompany the introduction of key documents that have implications for the practice of all agencies involved in child protection.** Such a commitment is needed if there is to be more than a paper commitment to a multi-agency approach.

- The means should be in place, either through ACPCs or LEAs, to record and monitor:
  - **the number of child protection referrals made by schools**
  - **the outcomes of school referrals**
  - **the attendance of representatives from schools at conferences involving school age children**
  - **the submission of written reports from schools at conferences involving school age children.**

LEAs would then be able to:

- identify areas of difficulty, potential training needs, and issues impeding effective multi-agency practice
- consider ways of increasing attendance rates at child protection meetings where this is appropriate.

- **Means need to be found to provide funding, specifically for supply cover, to allow school staff to attend conferences.** Not all LEAs will be able to do this within their present budgetary arrangements but discussions about how this could be achieved should be entered into with central Government.

- **Where specialist workers with a remit to attend all meetings are not in post ACPCs should consider the possibility of how such appointments could be facilitated.**

- **Urgent consideration should be given by LEAs, working in partnership with Social Services, as to how relationships between schools and local social-work teams may be improved and/or supported.** Given the number of authorities where relationships between Education and Social Services were said to be working well, while their schools complained of less satisfactory working relationships with local Teams, it is important to make sure that appropriate structures are in place. These would allow schools, when they have concerns, to access Managers in Social Services Departments, and Social Work Teams to contact the Education child protection service to inform the LEA when they consider that there has been a failure on the part of a school to act appropriately.

- **Schools should have access to reliable and informative guidance on how to deal with inappropriate sexual behaviour by pupils and peer abuse in its many forms.**

- **LEAs should make sure that clear guidelines are available for schools on when to approach parents for consent prior to making a referral to Social Services.**

- **There should be a co-ordinated approach across LEAs to ensure that those with child protection experience and those with curriculum responsibilities co-operate.** This liaison is important to ensure the availability of good quality materials to teach personal safety skills across all key stages. If these have not been developed within the authority there should be clear recommendations about appropriate resources.

- **It is vital that all teaching and non-teaching staff are aware of the correct procedures to be followed in relation to allegations made against any member of a school community.** This is in the interests of both children and adults.

- **The DfES should give careful consideration to increasing the number of Investigation and Referral Support Co-ordinators in post.** This is especially important if they are to be allowed to use their expertise in child protection to support the work of local authorities and to act in closer partnership with them.

References

Aldgate, J. And Tunstill, J. (1995). **Making Sense of Section 17: Implementing Services for Children in Need within the 1989 Children Act.** London: HMSO.

Audit Commission for Local Authorities in England and Wales and Ofsted. (2001). **Local Education Support for School Improvement.** London: Stationery Office.

Audit Commission for Local Authorities in England and Wales. (2001). **Schools' Views of their LEAs.** London: Audit Commission.

Baginsky, M. (2000). **Child Protection in Education.** London: NSPCC.

Baginsky, M. (2003). Newly qualified teachers and child protection. A survey of their views, training and experiences. **Child Abuse Review, Vol. 12.**

Baginsky, M. (forthcoming). A report on the relationship between schools and social services departments in relation to child protection referrals made by schools.

Children Act 1989. Chapter 41. London: HMSO.

Children (NI) Order 1995. Vol. 6. Belfast: Stationery Office.

Data Protection Act 1998. Chapter 29. London: Stationery Office.

Department for Education and Employment. (1995). **Protecting Children from Abuse: The Role of the Educational Service.** (Circular 10/95). London: DfEE Publications.

Department for Education and Skills. (2002). **Work Experience: a guide for secondary schools.** Sheffield: DfES.

Department for Education Northern Ireland. (1999). **Pastoral Care in Schools. Child Protection.** (Circular 1999/10). Belfast: DENI.

Department of Health. (1995). **Child Protection. Messages from Research.** London: HMSO.

Department of Health. (2001). **The Children Act Now. Messages from Research.** London: Stationery Office.

Department of Health. (2002). **Safeguarding Children: A Joint Chief Inspectors' Report on Arrangements to Safeguard Children.** London: Department of Health Publications.

Department of Health, Home Office and Department for Education and Employment. (1999). **Working Together to Safeguard Children: a guide to inter-agency working to**

safeguard and promote the welfare of children. London: Stationery Office.

Department of Health, Department for Education and Employment and Home Office. (2000). **Framework for the Assessment of Children in Need and their Families.** London: Stationery Office.

Derrington, C. (2000). **The LEA Contribution to School Improvement – A Role Worth Fighting for.** (LGA Research Report 9). Slough: NFER.

Education Act 2002. Chapter 32. London: Stationery Office.

Harris, A. (2001). Building capacity for school improvement. *School Leadership and Management,* Vol. 21, 261-70.

Her Majesty's Chief Inspector of Schools in England. (2002). **Framework for the Inspection of Local Education Authorities.** (Ref. HMI 345). Available from Ofsted: www.ofsted.gov.uk.

Human Rights Act 1998. Chapter 42. London: Stationery Office.

Local Authority Social Services Act 1970, Chapter 42. London: HMSO.

The National Assembly for Wales. (2000). **Working Together to Safeguard Children: a guide to inter-agency working to safeguard and promote the welfare of children.** Wales: National Assembly.
Cynulliad Cenedlaethol Cymru. (2000). **Gweithio Gyda'n Gilydd I Ddiogelu Plant: canllaw i weithio'n rhyngasiantaethol er mwyn diogelu a hyrwyddo lles plant.** Cymru: Cynulliad Cenedlaethol.

The National Assembly for Wales. (2001). **A Framework for Assessing Children in Need and their Families.** Wales: National Assembly.
Cynulliad Cenedlaethol Cymru. (2001). **Framwaith as gyfer Asesu Plant Angen a'u Teuluedd.** Cymru: Cynulliad Cenedlaethol.

Social Services Inspectorate. (1999). **Getting Family Support Right: Inspection of the Delivery of Family Support Services.** London: The Stationery Office.

Appendix 1: Welsh Local Education Authorities' Responses

Respondents

Fifteen of the 22 Welsh LEAs responded to the questionnaire. The respondents were:

3 Heads of School Improvement

3 Lead Officers for Child Protection

2 Assistant Directors

2 Senior Managers

1 Head of School Improvement

1 Learning Support Officer and one Special Educational Needs Officer

1 ESW Team Manager

1 Manager – Information Planning

1 Principal Educational Psychologist.

Guidance

All 15 LEAs provided guidance for their schools on child protection issues, but only three had posted it on their website.

Representation on ACPCs

All 15 Welsh LEAs were represented on their ACPCs and in 12 of them schools were also directly represented. There were comments similar to those made in England about how individuals represented the views of their colleagues and, in some cases, the difficulties of recruiting representatives:

> We sent out a request for volunteers and got one response!

Independent Schools

Seven of the 15 LEAs considered that they had some responsibility towards independent schools in relation to child protection issues. They were asked if they provided specific types of support in relation to child protection for independent schools and their replies are recorded in Table App. 1.1.

Table App. 1.1 LEA support for independent schools in relation to child protection – Wales

Source of support	No. of LEAs providing
Documentary guidance and information	4 of the 15
Child protection training	2 of the 15
Referral reporting route	3 of the 15
Professional advice	4 of the 15

The 15 respondents were asked to say if they checked maintained and independent schools in relation to the aspects recorded in Table App. 1.2.

Table App. 1.2 Oversight of maintained and independent schools in relation to child protection – Wales

Checks	LEA Schools	Independent schools
Written policies on child protection	14	2
Procedures in relation to child protection	15	2
Designated teachers with responsibility for child protection	15	2
Steps taken to communicate policies and procedures to all staff	15	2
A nominated governor with responsibility for child protection	8	0

Consultation service for LEA schools

All but two of the 15 LEAs were said to provide a child protection consultation service for their schools, usually through direct contact with the designated officer. One respondent stated that it came through a partnership with Social Services and through the County Council's legal department, and another said it was through the Education Welfare system. Twelve of the 13 providing this service included details of how to access it in the relevant documentation they sent to schools.

Training

All 15 responding LEAs included child protection training in their training programme for schools. Table App.1.3 records the groups for whom training is provided by these LEAs.

Table App. 1.3 Groups for whom LEAs provide child protection training – Wales

Training provided for:	No. of LEAs (n = 15)
Designated teachers	15
All teaching staff in schools	10
All staff in schools	12
Peripatetic staff	15
School governors	13
Classroom assistants	12
Learning mentors	6★

★ Not all LEAs would have Learning Mentors but it was not possible to determine from the responses how many of the other nine did have Mentors.

Most LEAs also referred to providing training for other professionals and groups including Educational Psychologists, Youth Workers, Sure Start staff, Family Support Workers, Education Welfare Officers, newly qualified and student teachers and many others coming into contact with school age children. However, three authorities did not make any such references.

Most respondents thought that schools were adequately, but not generously, funded for child protection training particularly as GEST has continued in Wales. One authority, for example, gives every primary school one day's teacher cover and every secondary school two days' cover to release staff specifically for child protection training each year.

- Twelve of the 15 LEAs responding to the questionnaire maintain a database that records the training each of their schools has received in relation to child protection.

- Twelve of the 15 LEAs maintain a database of the designated teachers in each of their schools. Eleven of the twelve were the same LEAs maintaining the database on training all schools had received, which leaves two LEAs which did not maintain either type of database.

- Ten of the 15 LEAs keep a record of the specific type of training undertaken by all staff in their schools.

- Eleven of the 15 LEAs had provided training on *Working Together to Safeguard Children* (The National Assembly for Wales, 2000) and 14 of the responding LEAs had done so on the *Framework for the Assessment of Children in Need and their Families* (The National Assembly for Wales, 2001).

- Eleven of the 15 LEAs were involved in other multi-agency training.

- Ten of the responding 15 LEAs provide specific funding for schools for supply cover to allow staff to attend child protection training.

- Seven of the 15 LEAs provide specific funding to support multi-agency training.

The main problems identified in relation to training reflect those which emerged in the responses from the English LEAs:

- the need for specified funding from the Government

- the failure of schools to be able to find supply teachers to cover for teachers on training

- the pressures under which schools operate.

A third of respondents referred to the difficulties faced by small, rural primary schools where there may be only two teachers on the staff and so it is difficult to release staff for training.

One respondent recognised that schools needed to prioritise training and, as there had been a relatively low turnover of designated teachers, the number attending basic training had diminished, while the demand for training of support staff had increased considerably.

Child protection conferences

- Ten of the 15 LEAs responding to the questionnaire keep a record of the number of child protection referrals which schools make to Social Services during the year.★

- Ten record the outcome of child protection referrals.★

- Ten record the proportion of conferences where schools are represented.

- Eight record the number of conferences where schools present a written report. It is only these eight responding LEAs which also record the other issues detailed above.

- Only one of the 15 LEAs provides earmarked funding for schools for supply cover to allow staff to attend child protection conferences.

- Eight respondents considered that schools and/or the Education Welfare Service represented the LEA at conferences; three LEAs sent an officer to as many conferences as possible and the other four did not consider that they would be represented. However, some of these LEAs, as well as those who thought they were represented, referred to other professionals, such as Educational Psychologists, attending in exceptional circumstances.

Impact of Framework for Assessment of Children in Need and their Families

Five respondents believed that the *Framework for Assessment* had had an effect on the LEA's involvement in child protection; six did not believe it had and four were not sure. Only four thought it had had an effect on schools' involvement in child protection, with five thinking it had not and the remaining six being uncertain.

Informing parents

Thirteen of the 15 respondents reported that the LEA and/or ACPC issued specific guidance on when and how to inform parents when the school makes a child protection referral. Most emphasised the need to obtain parental consent unless a child is *at risk of immediate harm*, with only two adding the importance of not jeopardising a future investigation.

Guidance on children and young people displaying inappropriate sexual behaviours

Eight of the LEAs produce guidance for schools in relation to children and young people displaying inappropriate sexual behaviours, with one more in the process of doing this. Four of the remaining six respondents thought that such guidance was necessary and should be produced.

★ Two respondents did add that the ACPC or Social Services maintained these records.

Guidance on dealing with peer abuse

Eight of the LEAs produce guidance for schools in relation to peer abuse and four of the remaining respondents thought that such guidance was necessary and should be produced.

Allegations against staff

The majority of respondents (13) have been involved in work designed to reduce the risk of a member of school staff being involved in an allegation of child abuse. All 15 have recommended to schools procedures for dealing with allegations of abuse against classroom teachers and head teachers.

Guidance in relation to other settings

Only five of the 15 responding LEAs produce guidance, policies or similar in relation to child protection in work placements used by school students and three do so in relation to other settings such as school trips, youth clubs, nurseries and sports facilities.

Working with professional associations/unions

Seven respondents reported that there had been joint working with professional associations and/or teaching unions in relation to the development of child protection policies and procedures; in four LEAs this had not happened and the remaining four respondents did not know if it had occurred.

Curriculum

Seven of the 15 responding LEAs had encouraged schools to teach personal safety skills in response to the duty on schools set out in Welsh Office Circular 52/92 in the Welsh PSE Framework. This was not being done in at least four of the remaining authorities, but the other four respondents did not know if other parts of the authority were undertaking such work.

Effectiveness of the system

Respondents were asked if, in their opinion, the present system for involving the key agencies in child protection worked. Twelve thought it did. The remaining three thought it did in part, but most referred to the system being more effective in relation to children *at risk* rather than those seen to be *in need*. Even those who viewed it in a positive light commented on the need for improvements within the agencies. These included a more consistent and reliable response from Social Services, the need for improved attendance at conferences and other meetings by GPs and recognition of the importance of involving other agencies when they have concerns. There were a few remarks about the possible effects of the shortage of experienced social workers around the country on this relationship. Four respondents referred to their perception that schools were sometimes reluctant to jeopardise their relationship with parents by making a referral. The solution was seen not only to lie in training but in opening the channels of communication and understanding between agencies, learning from 'past tragic mistakes' and making sure adequate resources were targeted on the area.

Respondents were also asked to give their views on whether, as a society, there was a system for protecting specific groups. Their views are reported in Table App.1. 4.

Table App. 1.4 Views on the system's ability to protect children – Wales

Group	Yes	No	Other★
Children of primary school age who are *at risk of significant harm*	12	–	3
Children of primary school age who are *in need*	9	2	4
Children of secondary school age who are *at risk of significant harm*	12	3	–
Children of secondary school age who are *in need*	9	2	4

★ Includes those who expressed uncertainty, referred to there being too much variation and those who failed to respond to this question.